ANDREA SANSOVINO

LONDON : HUMPHREY MILFORD

OXFORD UNIVERSITY PRESS

ANDREA SANSOVINO

Sculptor and Architect of the
Italian Renaissance

BY G. HAYDN HUNTLEY

1935
CAMBRIDGE
MASSACHUSETTS
HARVARD UNIVERSITY PRESS

PRINTED AT THE HARVARD UNIVERSITY PRESS

CAMBRIDGE, MASS., U. S. A.

TO

CHANDLER RATHFON POST

PREFACE

A STUDY on Andrea Sansovino needs no apology. Even the most summary histories of Italian art recognize his importance. Yet there has been but one attempt to evaluate his works as a whole since the time of Vasari. That was Schönfeld's little monograph, which was sympathetic and appreciative but which added little to Vasari's account. Moreover, articles in periodicals of scholarly pretension were surprisingly few. The most significant have been those by Fabriczy, Mauceri, and — very recently — Middeldorf. Semper and Stegmann with their collaborators wrote on some of Sansovino's architectural monuments and published valuable plates of photographs and measured drawings.

The hesitancy of scholars to study the *opus* of Sansovino has been due largely to three reasons: first, the difficulty of determining the work of any artist who was engaged on the adornment of the Santa Casa at Loreto; second, the necessity of investigating Sansovino's activities in Portugal; and third, a general lack of interest in the art of the sixteenth century.

The publication by an anonymous author in the *Civiltà Cattolica* of the documents of the Santa Casa which relate to Sansovino has been of greatest value to me, although I had previously succeeded in digging the facts concerning the sculpture from the archives of the sanctuary. I have taken the liberty of quoting many of the documents which were printed in the *Civiltà Cattolica* because of the inaccessibility of that publication to art scholars.

The reader will find in Chapter II the statement of an intensive and arduous investigation of Portugese and Spanish art in search of works by, or under the influence of, Sansovino. That the results of this search have been so negative I deeply regret, but such an investigation was a necessary prelude to any comprehensive study of the artist's life.

In the fervor and excitement of their discovery of the *quattrocento*, the art critics of the previous generation had a tendency to overlook the virtues of sixteenth-century art, which was often dismissed as vacuous and insincere. The art of the "primitives" is no longer a novelty crying for recognition; it is accepted and has become as "classic" to the critics of the younger generation as was the painting of Raphael to our grandfathers. So once again there is a certain interest in the art of the sixteenth century which extends beyond Michelangelo and Leonardo.

The reader may wonder why Sansovino never appears under the name of Contucci in these pages. Vasari used it, and Milanesi found that Andrea's sons called themselves Contucci, so that its use is certainly justifiable. But nowhere in documents or letters concerning Andrea was he ever called by that name, and I am inclined to believe that his sons adopted it only after his death. The increased wealth and social position of his family then demanded the use of a surname.

Appendix I is a chronological survey of Andrea's life. Some of the material is of questionable authority. Several of the dates are tentative and are included by the author in the hope that his understanding of the development of Sansovino's art may be helpful to students of the future. In all cases, full references are given to the source-material, and such words as "perhaps" and "probably" are used to indicate attribution or uncertainty.

I am indebted to kind people for assistance and encouragement in every step of my work, especially to the Contessina Gentilina Perozzi and the Conte Francesco Gianuizzi for aiding my research at Loreto. Dr. Ulrich Middeldorf has not only lent me the manuscript versions of unpublished articles on Sansovino's drawings, but has aided me in countless other ways. To Dr. Jenö

Lányi I am grateful for his insistence that there was something strange about the Corbinelli Altar. And finally, I must express my deep gratitude to Professor Chandler Rathfon Post and the Department of Fine Arts of Harvard University for making my study possible.

G. H. H.

WASHINGTON UNIVERSITY,
ST. LOUIS, MISSOURI
June 1, 1934

CONTENTS

LIST OF ILLUSTRATIONS

ANDREA SANSOVINO

I

THE EARLY LIFE AND TRAINING OF
ANDREA SANSOVINO

VASARI relates that Andrea was probably born in 1460. According to local tradition his birthplace is a farm called "Poggiolo," situated on the slopes of the Chiana Valley about a kilometer west of Monte San Savino. The testament of Nicolò di Menchi, Andrea's father, corroborates this tradition, for in it we find mentioned two pieces of property called "Maiale," properties which have been dependencies of Poggiolo until recent years. He was not ashamed of his humble origin, but rather sought opportunities to return to his native village. It is possible that the peasant house at Poggiolo is the same as that in which the sculptor was born. At all events, the little stone house, with a balcony, an open-air oven beside the steps, and a stable in the basement, must be similar to the home of the youthful Andrea.

The beginning of Sansovino's artistic career, as told by Vasari,[1] resembles the famous story of Giotto's discovery of Cimabue. One day while Andrea was herding cattle and was intent on drawing and modeling clay, Simone Vespucci, the Florentine *podestà* at Monte San Savino, passed by, and perceiving the boy's natural talent, asked his father's permission to take Andrea to Florence in order to give him that instruction which would develop his natural talents. The consent granted, Simone put the boy with Antonio del Pollajuolo.

Granted that Vasari has given his birth date correctly, Andrea must have entered Pollajuolo's shop about 1475. How long he remained with his master we do not know, but the training which he received there was thorough and the influence of his master may be traced throughout Sansovino's productions. In any case he must have served his apprenticeship under Antonio about 1475–1480; and it is likely that his connection with his master extended over a rather long period.

Doubtless, young Andrea di Nicolò had been in Florence only a brief time when the most splendid of *quattrocento* jousts took place in honor of Giuliano de' Medici, the younger brother of Lorenzo the Magnificent. On this occasion the handsome Giuliano wore a suit of silver armor. Indeed, it is said that his complete costume cost 8,000 florins. Both he and Lorenzo bore helmets designed by Verrocchio, who also painted Giuliano's standard. The tournament was further honored by one of the finest poems of the century, Politian's *La Giostra di Giuliano de' Medici*. This in turn inspired three of Botticelli's most famous paintings, *The Birth of Venus*, *Mars and Venus*, and the *Primavera*. What effect the joyous pageantry of a serenely happy Florence had upon the youth from Monte San Savino can only be surmised. Dare one explain the quiet and graceful art of Andrea by the influence of these years when he was young and impressionable? If so, one finds no reflection in his work of the tragic episode of 1478, when Giuliano was murdered, Lorenzo wounded, and Italy plunged into war. In the same year Monte San Savino, which was a frontier stronghold of the Florentines, capitulated to the combined forces of Naples and Rome.

Before penetrating into the career of Sansovino the artist let us have a brief look at Sansovino the man. "He was of rather small stature, but well formed and strong. His hair was long and silky, his eyes clear, nose aquiline, and skin white and ruddy. He had a slight impediment in his speech." [2] In the Palazzo Comunale at Monte San Savino is a sixteenth-century portrait of the artist which agrees well enough with Vasari's description. His

eyes were of that special Etruscan variety with very large pro-
tuberating eyeballs such as one sees in Piero dei Franceschi's
portrait of the Duke of Urbino.

In spite of his lowly birth, Andrea was fairly well educated, as
his letters and his interest in hydraulics and astronomy testify.
He must have acquired a fair education during his early years in
Florence, since he was much in the company of Bertoldo, the
learned Giuliano da San Gallo, and other brilliant men. His
hobby of astronomy and his invention of an astrolobe were fos-
tered by his sojourn in Portugal when that nation was in the heyday of her nautical discoveries. Vasari's word,[3] and two drawings,[4]
are our only testimonials of his accomplishments in this science.
In spite of the biographer's commendation [5] of his rare genius in
dealing with the difficulties of perspective, Sansovino never quite
learned what it was all about.

That he was of an amiable and generous disposition his rela-
tions with other artists prove. Between him and Jacopo Tatti
there is no sign of jealousy, although the younger man took his
name, and under it soon acquired a reputation superior to his
master's. His modesty and mild nature is well brought out in a
series of three letters [6] which he wrote in 1524 to Michelangelo,
with whom he sought work in a subordinate capacity. "I would
willingly serve you faithfully in everything that you command,
and this is because I have always liked you. . . . In brief, my
dear Michelangelo, you know and are acquainted with my ability
and how much I am worth, and thus, I offer to do whatsoever
will be your pleasure, not otherwise." Michelangelo did not
answer him. Andrea wrote twice more without receiving ac-
knowledgment.

There is only one record of a flash of temper on the part of
Sansovino. It was well justified. The story, as told by Vasari,[7]
follows:

The pope sent him [Baccio Bandinelli] to Loreto, for Andrea to give him one of the reliefs. But Baccio began to criticize Andrea's works and those of the other sculptors there, and said that they did not know how to design. Soon they all disliked him. When Andrea heard what Baccio had said of him, he reprimanded him gently, like a wise man, saying that work is done with the hands and not with the tongue, and that good design is not to be judged by drawings but in the perfection of the finished work in stone. He concluded by saying that Baccio must speak of him more respectfully in the future. But as Baccio replied with many abusive words, Andrea could bear no more, and tried to kill him. They were separated by others who were present. Baccio had to go to Ancona to carry on his work.

A brief survey of the activities of Antonio Pollajuolo during these years affords a rough idea of the training Sansovino received in his shop. *The Martyrdom of St. Sebastian* in the National Gallery dates from 1475, and other paintings by Antonio from the same time are the *Rape of Deianira* in the Jarvis collection at New Haven, and the two small Hercules panels in the Uffizi. "Indeed 1475 is the last date we have for Antonio's activity as a painter, whereas numerous documents of later date record his plastic work in metal. We can be almost certain that after his departure for Rome in 1484, he laid aside his paints and brush." This characterization by Van Marle [8] of Antonio's activity during this decade is most interesting in relation to the master's influence upon his most distinguished pupil. Sansovino's drawing of *St. Joseph* (Fig. 67) clearly demonstrates that he adopted from Antonio the painter his type of Val d'Arno landscape. From about the same time come the famous engraving, *The Battle of the Nudes*, and the splendid drawing of nude warriors in the P. J. Sachs collection, both of which furnish comparisons for certain of Andrea's reliefs. To the year 1477 is ascribed Pollajuolo's relief of the *Nativity of St. John the Baptist* on the silver altar for the baptistry. The fact that Antonio was working in relief when Andrea was beginning his studies may well account for Sansovino's predilection for that mode of expression. The small bronze group of *Hercules and*

Antaeus in the Bargello is generally dated about 1480. Of particular interest in regard to a battle-piece which Sansovino did for the King of Portugal is Vasari's account[9] of how after Antonio's death "a model was discovered for an equestrian statue of Francesco Sforza, Duke of Milan, which he did for Ludovico. There are two versions of this in our book: in the one Verona is represented beneath, in the other the figure is in full armour, and on a pedestal full of battle scenes he makes the horse tread upon an armed man." Leonardo, as well as Sansovino, may have borrowed from these designs.

Antonio Pollajuolo's great qualities, "that union of force and grace, of antique stability and renaissance motion,"[10] as well as his establishment of a new scientific and artistic anatomy, were qualities which his sculptor-pupil took over and modified to suit his own more serene and plastic style.

Until Dr. Middeldorf began discovering drawings of Andrea Sansovino the direct and undiluted influence of Pollajuolo in that master's early work passed unnoticed. The characteristics and types common to both artists will receive consideration as they appear in the works of Sansovino.

The Galba Plaque

In his life of Andrea Sansovino Vasari implies that from this early period in Pollajuolo's shop came two terra-cotta heads of the Emperors Galba and Nero made to decorate a chimney-piece in the house of Simone Vespucci. In his second edition the famous biographer adds that "the *Galba* is now in the house of Giorgio Vasari at Arezzo." And, of a truth, the modern visitor to Vasari's house will see a plaque of Galba (Fig. 1) like that described above. The emperor, portrayed as a bust in profile facing the right, is wearing a wreath of leaves and a toga which is secured over his right shoulder by a dull red button. The portrait so completely fills the placque that the wreath and toga project over the simple frame-moulding. The relief is low and of a soft, undulating quality well chosen for the subject as well as the material. Clear, bright glazes, similar to those used in Italian renaissance faïence, color the clay surface. Whether this happy addition was intended by the artist, we are not told; but from the harmony of the modeling in color with that in clay, it seems likely that the color was applied by the sculptor or under his supervision. The features of the emperor were probably taken from a Roman coin, perhaps a *sestertius*, of which Vespasian struck several about 71 A.D. in order to win the good will of the Senate by restoring that body's favorite, Galba, to honor. They show the same wreath tied with a ribbon at the base of the skull, the same features, and, of course, are in similar flat relief. Such portraits adapted from ancient coins appear on the bases of the *putti*-flanked candelabra done by Benedetto da Majano for the Sala dell'Orologia in the Palazzo Vecchio. These must date from the period of 1475 to 1481, and are, therefore, probably from the same time as Andrea's. Such adaptions of antique coins are frequent in fifteenth-century sculpture.

The Altar of the Madonna in Sta. Chiara at Monte San Savino

The earliest of Sansovino's important works which have come down to us is an altar of the Virgin enthroned, now in the church of Sta. Chiara at Monte San Savino (Fig. 2), although it was made for the chapel of the suppressed convent of St. 'Agatha. Vasari describes it as "the Assumption with St. Agatha, St. Lucy, and St. Romuald [there are four saints]; it was glazed by the della Robbia."[11] The subject is, in fact, the old *motif* of the Madonna and Child in a glory with saints and angels, a *motif* not too popular in fifteenth-century Florence, which preferred to seat the Madonna on a substantial throne.

Mary, surrounded by cherubim heads, is seated in the clouds. She looks down on the nearly nude Christ Child sitting on her left knee. He, in turn, is blessing the two saints who kneel adoring on the step below. Beside these kneeling figures, who enhance the internal unity of the composition by having their backs turned toward the spectator, stand two saints in niches, like statues that are insensible to the vision which is taking place beside them. The female saint in the niche to the left holds at hip level a book in her left hand and some object over her breast in her right hand. Her eyes gaze musingly into the distance; her face has that pensive expression so dear to the masters of the late *quattrocento*. Opposite her, in the right-hand niche, is a firm-willed and strong-bodied monk, completely absorbed in a book which he holds in both hands. His left forearm sustains a scourge against his chest and upper arm. In the violet-colored arch which continues the fields of the niches of the same hue, two slender flying angels descend with a garlanded crown for the Queen of Heaven. In the taste of the time, fruit and flowers are gathered and tied into bunches to decorate the pilasters and the arch over them.

The architectural and perspective construction of the altarpiece is peculiar and a bit confusing. Seemingly Sansovino was influenced by a pictorial composition of the type of the *Santa Conversazione* in the Uffizi (No. 8388) by Ghirlandajo. In adapting such an idea to the medium of terra-cotta and the desired frame, Andrea renounced the terrestrial setting, put the Madonna in a glory, the standing saints in niches, which are really a part of the frame, and set the angels in the corresponding field of the tympanum. The result was to create a sort of altar-within-an-altar, for the kneeling saints appear to be worshipping at a shrine which is composed of all the other figures. In carrying out this unusual conception the sculptor might have succeeded better had

he made the adoring figures larger — they are somewhat larger
than the niche saints — and used a lower relief for the rest of the
altar. Probably this lack of definition of the different roles of the
two groups of figures was a deliberate choice on the part of Sansovino, an artistic license taken to achieve a greater unity of the
whole. That it was so is borne out by a comparison with Masaccio's similar conception in his fresco of *The Trinity, St. John the
Evangelist, Mary and Donors* in Sta. Maria Novella. There the
donors worship before a shrine containing the holy figures; the
problem was the same as in the Monte San Savino sculpture, and
the solution was identical.

Since Monte San Savino is not far distant from Siena, it is of
interest to note that pictorial parallels to this composition are to
be found in Sienese painting which are closer than the above-
mentioned altar by Ghirlandajo. Especially pertinent is the
Madonna delle Nevi (dated 1477) by Matteo di Giovanni, a
painter who must have passed through Monte San Savino many
times on his journeys from Siena to Borgo San Sepolcro, his native city.

Critics by no means have agreed with Vasari's attribution of
this altar to Andrea Sansovino: Fischer [12] called it a work of Cozzarelli; Schönfeld [13] excluded it from the productions of Sansovino
because of the facial types and drapery treatment; Burckhardt in
the *Cicerone* also said that it was Sienese; and Fabriczy [14] affirmed
that it was a work of the mature *cinquecento*. Fabriczy pointed
out that the altar Vasari described was not in Sta. Chiara, that it
was an *Assumption*, and that it had only three saints, whereas
this has four. It is, indeed, surprising to find the discoverer of
the Sta. Margherita tabernacle (Fabriczy) failing to recognize the
many elements of Andrea's style in this altar. Dr. Middeldorf [15]
demonstrated similarities of technique in the *Galba* plaque and
in the cherubim heads of this altar, and also found analogies in

facial types and drapery handling with the two drawings in the Uffizi. Reasons for dating the Sta. Chiara altar about 1480 are: first, its resemblance to the paintings of Ghirlandajo and Cozzarelli above mentioned and to many others of that time; second, the elongated proportions of the angels and the standing female saint, whose head-dress, small high breasts, narrow waist, and jug-like abdomen vividly recall Pollajuolo's work on the silver altar for the baptistry and also remind one of Botticelli's graceful feminine creations; and third, the fine sentiment expressed in attitudes and faces is characteristic of Florentine art in the heyday of Lorenzo the Magnificent. The thinness of the architecture of the niches is to be found in Sansovino's other altar (Fig. 18) in the same church and likewise in the drawing of *Astronomy* (Fig. 68), while the curious perspective treatment is repeated not only in that drawing but also in the sculptor's latest reliefs (Fig. 50) at Loreto. That this altar belongs to the earliest period of Andrea's activity is borne out by a study of the facial types of the two angels: that on the left is Pollajuolesque and may almost be duplicated on the tomb of Sixtus IV (the head of Grammatica); that on the right is the same type used on the Corbinelli altar. Or compare the cherubim heads with those on the Sto. Spirito altar, and the expression of that cherubim above the kneeling male saint's hand with the St. John (Fig. 17) of the Corbinelli work on one hand, and with various agonizing heads of Pollajuolo on the other. Consider also the similarity of the hands and the way the folds of the cloak fall in the St. James (Fig. 12) of the Florentine altar and the female saint to the left here. Indeed, the facial types of the two figures are the same, with straight mouths, thin noses, pinched-in nostrils, and much exposed upper eyelids. A peculiarity of Sansovino so marked that it might almost be considered a signature is here present in a high degree: it is the rhythmic meandering line which may be found around the waist of the standing woman and in various edges of the angels' drapery. Some of the other appearances of this are in the flying drapery of the angels (Fig. 6) on the Sta. Margherita tabernacle, in the drapery above the right ankle of St. James (Fig. 12) in Sto. Spirito, in the cloud *motifs* of the Madonna reliefs on the Sta. Maria del Popolo tombs (Fig. 37), and in the *Annunciation* (Fig. 50) at Loreto. I have taken some pains to prove the attribution and approximate date of this altar, not only because both have been questioned by critics, but also to establish a basis for determining the earliest style of Sansovino, a style of great beauty which justifies Sansovino's being given a high rank as a *quattrocentista*.

Returning to Vasari's statement, I find that his identification of three of the saints is as well founded as any other I might offer. Is it possible that the kneeling saint with a church beside him is St. Sabin? The identification of the standing saint to the left as Agatha is reasonable since the altar was in a church dedicated to that saint, but the attributes are unusual, indeed what she has in her left hand I do not know unless it be the central portion of a pair of shears. The kneeling saint with the torch may well be Lucy, although St. Genevieve is sometimes represented veiled and bearing a torch. She is, however, infrequently seen in Italian art. The identification of St. Romuald is the most satisfactory of the four, not only because he is the right type with correct attributes and dress, but also because of the proximity of Camaldoli. That the terra-cotta was glazed by the della Robbia has never been challenged — the colors and glazes substantiate Vasari's words. The fruit-garlanded frame is closely related to similar *motifs* of the della Robbia.

The Tabernacle of Sta. Margherita in Montici

About two miles to the south of Florence, beyond the Pian de' Giullari, and high above San Miniato al Monte, the simple and

ancient church of Sta. Margherita crowns the highest summit of
those delightful hills which lie between the Val d'Ema and the Val
d'Arno. In the choir to the left of the high altar, the usual place,
one finds a small marble tabernacle (Fig. 3) set in the wall as a
repository for the *oleum sacrum*. It is of the type established in
quattrocento Florence by Bernardo Rossellino.[16] From a small
podium, decorated with the symbols of the Evangelists on swing-
ing garlands, rise two arabesqued pilasters which bear an entablature and enclose an arch, within which are two angels and a perspective vestibule that leads up to the little door. There are two
cherubim heads in the spandrels, and in the central lunette of the
perspective-treated compartment is the symbol of the Holy Ghost.

Fabriczy discovered this work and attributed it to the late
fifteenth century, and — largely by a process of elimination — to
Andrea Sansovino. The date we do not know, but I am inclined
to believe that it was done at about the time that Andrea was
beginning the altar for Sto. Spirito. The cherubim heads (Fig. 4)
in execution and expression closely resemble those of the Corbinelli altar but in type are the same as those on the polychro-
matic altar at Monte San Savino. The proportions and unity of
the architecture (which Fabriczy praises), as well as the carving
of the ornament, are indeed similar to those of the Florentine altar
and of the same high quality. The angels (Figs. 5 and 6) are admirably and forcibly carved in spite of the difficulties which their
perspective setting engendered. As with the cherubim heads, so
too do these figures exhibit characteristics intermediate between
the angels of the early terra-cotta altar and the Gabriel and spandrel genii of the Corbinelli altar (Fig. 11). The resemblance to
the spandrel figures is striking in many ways — anatomy, drapery, hair, and nervous tension. They lack the sureness of touch
and anatomical coordination of the figures in the predella scenes
of the large altar.

The Corbinelli Altar

Matteo Corbinelli in his last will and testament, dated February 22, 1420, set aside property with the Arte di Lana to keep up the family altar of the Holy Sacrament in the church of Santo Spirito. On December 13, 1485, the chapter of the convent of Santo Spirito granted the Corbinelli family, according to their ancient privilege, the chapel of the Sacrament in the new basilica.[17] It is probable, and in accord with the artistic development of Sansovino, that he began the altar, which Vasari attributes to him, shortly after the above grant.

The altar itself is to be found in the central chapel of the left transept, a chapel of which the private ownership is asserted by a semicircular wooden balustrade of late date. As one sees it today (Fig. 7) the chapel has four main features: first, the reredos, of a form suggesting the arch of Constantine, with a tabernacle in the central opening, statues in the side apertures, and a figure of the Christ Child in a broken pediment as a central, crowning *motif*; second, the altar-table with a frontal adorned by a bas-relief of the *Pietà*; third, the pilastered revetment which continues the order of the reredos around the curving walls of the chapel; and last, the marble balustrade which bears the date 1642, and replaces the bronze railing noted by Vasari.

The style of this altar and its chapel has disturbed various critics. Burckhardt[18] believed that the reliefs of the Coronation of Mary, the Annunciation, and the *Pietà* were either much earlier than the rest of the sculpture or out of the school of Mino or Rossellino. Schönfeld[19] pointed out that the *Pietà* relief differed from the other reliefs in mode of treatment, that the heads have vertical instead of perspective halos, and that here only have the eyes drilled pupils; accordingly he concluded that the altar frontal was not by Andrea Sansovino. Likewise, Schönfeld recognized that the pilastered revetment at the sides of the reredos differed in style from the architectural carving of the altar, and that the jointing between the altar and the wall revetment was awkward; therefore he suggested that the year 1642 — carved on the chapel railing — was the date of this work. Spurred on by the doubts of these careful critics and aided by Dr. Lányi, after a most careful examination I found that the altar had been at least partially rebuilt, and that the chapel contains the work of three different epochs. Figure 8 shows the altar reconstructed as Sansovino must have left it about 1490. Let us compare it with an unretouched photograph (Fig. 7). The broken pediment and the entire superstructure above the Coronation relief have been removed, the curving frieze of angel heads and the Dove continued into a semicircle, and the Christ Child set at the apex of this rounded attic. This reordination is proved (see Fig. 9), first, by the rounded base of the block under the Child; second, by the patently broken and misarranged frieze of cherubim heads, where the wings do not fit the heads and where at the lower extremities two pieces of wings have no function; third, by the style of the mouldings (clearly seventeenth century), the broken pediment, and the seventeenth-century floral arabesques which are repeated exactly on the balustrade below (which is also of the same bluish marble, quite different from the warm-toned marble used by Sansovino); and fourth, on the analogy of later altars which took it as a model (the altar (Fig. 10) from S. Girolamo, Fiesole, by Andrea Ferrucci, now in the Victoria and Albert Museum, London; an altar in S. Medardo, Arcevia, by Giovanni della Robbia, dated 1513 [20]; and an altar in S. Lucchese, Poggibonsi, school of Giovanni della Robbia, dated 1514 [21]). Also the backgrounds of the three upper reliefs have been darkened to represent the colored marble or stucco, the former presence of which is indicated not only by the very rough state of the marble in those places, but also by the demands of the composition both within the reliefs themselves and in their relation to the colored marbles of the arched niches below. Furthermore, it seems, although all traces have disappeared, that the mouldings and arabesques were gilded and that the predella reliefs were touched up with color or gilding. The altar by Ferrucci (Fig. 10) preserves its polychromy in all these particulars. The marble revetment of the chapel walls is decorated with arabesqued pilasters and panels carved in a style which harmonizes well enough with the style of the altar, but which shows an altogether different hand. Moreover, the character of the arabesques would date the revetment in the first decade of the sixteenth century. On the first pilaster to the left of the altar, at the height of the impost moulding, Dr. Lányi called to my attention a small plaque carved with the device of a dolphin crossed by a trident. To be sure, neither dolphins nor tridents separately or both together are rare in renaissance decoration; and I never should have considered this placque of any importance had I not found precisely similar devices on the basement of the Basso tomb in Santa Maria del Popolo, Rome. In both instances the occurrence of this *motif* appears awkward, as if it had been forced into the design. Although dolphins and tridents are not uncommon in Sansovino's decorative work, these are the only monuments in which they are used in such a way, as a device. The date of execution of the Basso tomb (1505–1509) agrees with the style of the arabesque carvings on the Santo Spirito chapel walls. It may be that the same *scarpellino* had executed both the Florentine work and the decoration of the Roman tomb; or, what is more likely, that Sansovino adopted this device as a sort of signature, and that the Santo Spirito paneling was executed from his designs. The failure of this device to reappear in his later works may be explained by the fact that he ceased to use arabesque decoration. In its general effect this continuation of the order around the chapel is happy enough, although the horizontality must have been oppressive before the seventeenth-century additions to the altar attic; in detail, one may criticize unfavorably the extreme flatness of the entablature continuation, the dull carving of the capitals, the meaningless prolongation of the impost moulding, and the broad, unbroken sweep of the predella band which destroys the continuity between the vertical lines of the pilasters and the basement membering. Other alterations which have been made include the substitution of a new gilded bronze door to the tabernacle of the host, a new Crucifixion above it, and the moving forward of the tabernacle in its niche in order to make it accessible after the depth of the mensola had been rudely increased. There are signs of breakage — the wing of Gabriel, the arm of the left spandrel figure, various nicks in the left central pilaster, one of St. James' toes, his staff, and the aforementioned semicircular band of angel heads — which lead one to think that the altar must have suffered an accident, perhaps from lightning, which required the rebuilding in 1642. Such an accident, however, hardly explains the disappearance of the bronze candelabra and railing mentioned by Vasari.

This altar, executed during the last years of Lorenzo de' Medici's glorious rule, this work which made the fame of Andrea, is of such importance as a touchstone for identifying his earlier works and for judging the development of his style that it seems best to consider it detail by detail from several points of view.

One finds precedent for the use of the three-bayed triumphal arch *motif* as an altar in Rome; for example, an altar in S. Gregorio Magno, dated 1468, which has most of the elements of this reredos, including the semicircular attic, but without the Christ Child. Also one finds that Antonio Rossellino used a similar composition for the altar of the *Adoration* in the church of Monte Oliveto, Naples. In the same church of Monte Oliveto, Benedetto da Majano was building an altar of this general type while Andrea was executing the Corbinelli commission in Florence.

But of all the possible prototypes for this altar that which seems most significant — in spite of the fact that it is but a single arch in width — is the marble tabernacle by Desiderio da Settignano in San Lorenzo. This must be anterior to 1464, the year of Desiderio's death. It, too, is a shrine for the host, and has a relief of the *Pietà* as a frontal, but what is most pertinent is the treatment of the pediment with an arched cornice broken by a figure of the blessing nude Christ Child. Furthermore, there are architectural similarities in these altars of Desiderio and Andrea, both of which happen to be in churches designed by Brunelleschi.

The decorative carving is of great delicacy and originality. The capitals are made up of three crisp-fronded acanthus leaves surmounted by a *fleuron* and two larger leaves which are coerced into spiral forms by cords that are visible on the scrolls. The decorative carving on the pilasters is in harmony with the mode of execution of the reliefs of the Annunciation. The pilaster reliefs represent the Dove supporting by ribbons various instruments of the Passion — subjects that are appropriate for an altar of the Sacrament. Below the pilasters the two inner podia are carved with voluted, crossed torches, while the two outer podia have over the crossed torches superimposed shields with exquisitely modeled stags, the arms of the Corbinelli. These stags, in violation of the usage of heraldry, are turned one to the left, the other to the right, for the sake of symmetry.

The figure of the blessing Christ Child (Fig. 9) at the apex of the tomb bears a general resemblance to the infant Christs of Verrocchio (especially He of the marble relief in the Bargello), of Antonio Rossellino, and of Benedetto da Majano; but the anatomic lines and facial expression are original with Sansovino. The greatest innovation, however, is the plastic fullness attained largely through broad surface modeling and heightened by the cloak, which falls diagonally from the right hip to the left ankle in a line recalling Ghiberti's graceful draperies. While the drapery and attitude differ, this is substantially the same child that appears on the glazed altar in Monte San Savino.

The candelabrum-bearing angels, the most *cinquecento* elements of the altar, are not far removed from those used on the Sforza and Basso tombs, despite their Pollajuolesque sweeping movement and strong linear quality.

Historians and critics of sculpture have seized on Andrea in the character of the first sculptor of the High Renaissance to such an extent that they have generally overlooked the fact that his work in the fifteenth century includes some of the finest *quattrocento* sculpture of Florence. Such a piece is the relief of the Coronation of the Virgin (Fig. 9). In the beautiful handling of drapery, which combines the graceful lines of Ghiberti and the structure-revealing qualities of Pollajuolo and Verrocchio, Sansovino excels other *quattrocento* masters. Mary is of the fine type Andrea developed during these years. She has an intensity and sincerity of expression worthy of Donatello — qualities that one does not expect to find in Andrea — and a humility befitting a St. Catherine of Siena. The surrounding cherubim heads complete this masterpiece of *quattrocento* sweetness and tenderness. Yet when one compares this with contemporary representations of the subject, such as the *Coronation of the Virgin* by Piero Pollajuolo in the Collegiata at S. Gimignano, one finds a striking contrast between the elongated figures of Piero and the stocky, compact bodies of Andrea — an indication that Andrea is already breaking with the tradition of his masters. In such a comparison, too, one is surprised to see that Sansovino has chosen the bearded figure of God the Father rather than Christ, the more traditional character. The Holy Ghost is the dove with a nimbus in the frieze above. This type of God the Father will reappear in Sansovino's repertory in S. Maria del Popolo and even as late as 1518 in the *Annunciation* at Loreto.

Above the side niches with the Apostles are two *tondi* (Figs. 11 and 12) containing low reliefs of Gabriel bringing his holy message, and the Virgin Annunciate. As I mentioned above, I am convinced that the backgrounds of these reliefs were filled in with a dark-colored marble or imitation of such marble in stucco. Reliefs bearing such a resemblance to *opus sectile* would be unusual, but not without precedent in the sculpture of Donatello. In another respect, that is the low vanishing point of the perspective, these reliefs are out of the ordinary. By choosing a vanishing point in the center of the altar Sansovino not only creates an illusion of scenes above one's head (compare Mantegna's frescoes in the Eremitani and the altar in San Zeno), but also achieves a more unified composition by drawing these strong, if invisible, lines to converge on the shrine of the Sacrament. The very decorative effect of the left *tondo* is enhanced by the rich patterns of the bouquet of lilies and the scroll-tipped wings. There in the broad, open arcade the tone is of quiet confidence. The complicated architecture and fancy furniture of the *tondo* of the Virgin accentuate her surprise and anxiety at receiving the divine charge.

The Evangelist, St. Matthew (Fig. 11), in the left niche, is the type of Ciuffagni and Ghiberti brought up to date. The tousled hair, the questioning eyes, the pinched nose, the short beard, and the garb of toga and Roman sandals are found in the statues of all three sculptors. Even the idea of the brass halo may have been suggested by those of the cathedral Evangelists of the early *quattrocento*. A comparison with Ghiberti's St. Matthew (on Or San Michele) is valuable as emphasizing the differences of the times. The head of the later statue is much larger in proportion to the body. Both figures stand on one foot; Sansovino's is static, whereas Ghiberti's appears to be sidestepping. The drapery of the earlier statue is arranged in harmonies of "dish folds," and falls in lines which are straight or only slightly curving. The garment edges are carved in simple, almost mathematical, curves. The drapery serves a tectonic purpose. In the Sto. Spirito Matthew the folds are not straight or evenly curving, but everywhere there is the variation of nature; and surfaces, instead of being plane, are undulating to produce shadows which bring out the underlying form. In other words, the treatment is plastic. Other plastic indications are the rounded, closed outline, which even includes the feet, the holding in of the hands as compared with the Ghiberti statue, and the massy treatment of hair. The hands are the thick-palmed, knotty-jointed hands which Andrea learned to draw in the studio of Antonio Pollajuolo. Sansovino's characterization of Matthew and James as inspired day-laborers was achieved largely by the use of this arthritic type of hand. The symbols which Matthew is holding are an open book and an inkhorn, the top of which is a lumpy piece of lead.

The St. James (Fig. 12) was cut from a faulty block of marble which has turned altogether too yellow, but which in some places, notably the mouth, has remained unpleasantly white. Photographs accentuate this color difference. James is shown reading aloud from a book which he holds in his open hand. In his left hand he holds a fragment of a pilgrimage staff. His right foot protrudes over the ledge of the niche. The folds over the raised leg have a peculiar bronze-like quality which reminds one of Verrocchio.

Under the statue of St. Matthew is a decollation scene (Fig. 11) that, one may be sure, represents the martyrdom of Matthew. The scene does not accord with the story told in the *Golden Legend*.[22] There the executioner strikes the Apostle from behind while he stands in prayer before an altar, with his arms extended toward heaven.

The mode of relief (Fig. 13), although less pictorial, is similar to that of the monument of S. Savino in the cathedral of Faenza, or the pulpit by Benedetto da Majano in Sta. Croce, but there are many important differences. The perspective does not mount so rapidly, the actual depth of the carving is greater, the number of planes is reduced to two in the immediate foreground, and finally, the figures are so detached from the background that they cast shadows and one feels the air which actually surrounds them. To this relief (Fig. 14) most especially does Vasari's praise apply: "They are so well wrought that the brush's point could hardly do what Andrea has done with the chisel."[23]

The Last Supper (Fig. 15), which is appropriately placed below the tabernacle of the Sacrament, is of interest as being intermediate in date between Ghirlandajo's in the Ognissanti refectory and Leonardo's in Milan. The actors are more agitated and better grouped, the scene is more dramatic, and the composition more concentrated than in the earlier example, but in all these respects it is far inferior to the *Cena* in the refectory of Sta. Maria delle Grazie. In keeping with the purpose of the altar which it adorns, the relief's central figure is Christ comforting St. John and blessing the Bread.

The third predella piece (Fig. 12) depicts an incident in the life of St. James as related in the *Golden Legend*:[24]

While he was preaching the word of God in Judea, a magician named Hermogenes, in accord with the Pharisees, sent one of his disciples, Philetus, to prove to St. James that what he spoke was untrue. But the Apostle defeated him before a crowd of people with irrefutable proofs and numerous miracles, so that Philetus returned to Hermogenes, upholding the doctrine of St. James. He recounted the miracles worked by the saint, declared he wished to become his disciple, and exhorted Hermogenes to imitate him. But Hermogenes in anger bound him so fast by his magic that he could not move a limb. "We will see," he said, "if your St. James will free you." After Philetus had informed James of this through his servant, the Apostle sent him his cloak and said, "The Lord upholdeth all that fall, and raiseth up all those that be bowed down" [Ps. CXLV]. As soon as Philetus was touched with the cloak, he was freed of his chains, and mocking at the sorcery of Hermogenes, he hastened to join St. James. Hermogenes in fury convoked his demons and ordered them to fetch him James bound together with Philetus, in order to avenge himself on them, so that in the future the Apostle's disciples would not dare to insult him. Now when they approached St. James, the demons began to howl in the air, and said, "James, Apostle, take pity on us, for we burn before our time is come." St. James replied, "Why have you come to me?" They answered, "Hermogenes sent us to fetch you and Philetus; but hardly had we started toward you when the angel of God tied us with chains of fire and tortured us sorely." "If the angel of the Lord is to untie you," replied the Apostle, "return to Hermogenes and bring him to me bound, but without harm to him." Then they seized Hermogenes, tied his hands behind his back and brought him thus bound to St. James, saying, "Where you have sent us we have been burned and horribly tortured." And the demons said to St. James, "Put him under our power, so we may avenge the wrong he has done you, and the fire which burnt us." St. James said to them, "Here is Philetus before you, why don't you take him?" The demons replied, "We cannot even lay hand on an ant in your chamber." St. James then said to Philetus, "In order to return good for evil, according to the teaching of Jesus Christ, since Hermogenes tied you, you untie him." When Hermogenes was free he was ashamed, and St. James said to him, "Go freely where you wish, for it is not our principle to convert one in spite of himself." Hermogenes answered, "I know too well the fury of the demons. If you do not give me an object to carry with me, they will kill me." St. James gave him his staff, then Hermogenes fetched all of his books of magic before the Apostle for him to burn them. But St. James, for fear that the odor of this fire would inconvenience those who were not on their guard, ordered him to throw them in the sea. When he had returned, Hermogenes prostrated himself before the Apostle and said, "Liberator of souls, receive a penitent whom you have spared thus far, although he was envious and a calumniator."

Sansovino has dramatized the moment when St. James turns to Philetus and says, "Since Hermogenes tied you, you untie him." To fill out the long space a third figure, perhaps the servant of Philetus, is introduced. The torture and writhing of Hermogenes and the demons is represented with such skill that one searches for prototypes, especially on the Etruscan cinerary urns. But such search has been in vain. Also, the subject is not common in art.

Most fitting as the decoration for the frontal of an altar dedicated to the Holy Sacrament is the devotional *Pietà*, here treated as the pictorial symbol of the *Corpus Christi*. The full effect of this illusionistic relief can be had only by kneeling at the altar railing. From that position Mary and John appear to be standing behind a low parapet that hides the nether part of their legs (compare Ghirlandajo's frescoes in the Sassetti chapel of Sta. Trinità). The half-draped legs of Christ are admirably foreshortened, although — as was generally the case at that time, and for some years later — lacking in perspective gradations of size. A device which assists in developing the illusionary effect is the bringing forward of the base moulding under the sarcophagus. An interesting prototype of this *Pietà* occurs on the tomb of Bishop Federighi by Luca della Robbia, in Sta. Trinità. There each figure is in a separate panel and Mary and John are quieter, yet the pious, resigned expression of Christ is the same and the Madonna and John are in attitudes similar to those used by Sansovino. An example of this subject which unites the three figures and has a more intense emotional expression is the relief under the *Madonna dell'Ulivo* by Benedetto da Majano in the cathedral of Prato.

As I have said previously, Schönfeld believed this to be a later work and probably not by Andrea Sansovino. Nor has he been alone in that opinion; it has been suggested that the youthful Jacopo Sansovino was the author because of the Madonna type and because of the analogies between the head of John the Evangelist and Jacopo's *Bacchus*. In view of this prevalent doubt I shall attempt to show that the relief is by Andrea and that it was done while he was still closely under the influence of Pollajuolo.

A profile view of the head of St. John affords undeniable proof of a close relationship with the art of Antonio Pollajuolo. A superficial comparison of this photograph and the heads of the warriors in Pollajuolo's famous engraving demonstrates a similarity not only in line and feeling but also in details, such as the way of wrinkling the forehead, the representation of tenseness in the nostrils and lips, the drawing of teeth and tongue, and the treatment of hair. The hands resemble those used by Antonio in his painting of *Hercules Slaying Antaeus* (Uffizi), the Uffizi drawings of *Adam* and *Eve*, and many other works. Likewise, the anatomy of the Christ is so similar to that of Adam in Pollajuolo's drawing that if Pollajuolo were unknown an attribution of the Uffizi drawing to Sansovino would be excusable. The treatment of the drapery, especially in the Virgin's hood and the loin cloth of Christ, adds proof to my contention that the relief of the *Pietà* is by Andrea Sansovino, and that it is so close to Antonio Pollajuolo's style that it must be dated before Andrea's trip to Portugal.

The floor of the chapel is made of green and white marble tiles. The front of the step on which the altar-table rests is incised with a foliate pattern of which the furrows undoubtedly were filled with a *niello* preparation, of which traces remain.

Sansovino and Bertoldo

Florence in the fifteenth century was a hotbed of enthusiasm for the antique. Humanists and poets extolled the culture of the ancients; scholars discovered and transcribed antique manuscripts; and patrons of learning and art demanded not only literature in the antique fashion but also statues, paintings, and buildings. Yet it may be said that, with few exceptions, the architects, sculptors, and painters of the *quattrocento* were incapable of creating in the spirit of antiquity. Botticelli's *Birth of*

Venus illustrates this point. And Verrocchio in the *Baptism* and the *Doubting of Thomas* is far closer in feeling to the art of fifteenth-century Flanders than to the art of Greece and Rome. Toward the end of the century, however, the precepts of thinkers like Alberti, Brunelleschi, and Mantegna began to take root firmly in fertile soil and produced a generation of artists who from their earliest teachings thought in terms of the antique. That was the generation of Michelangelo, of Fra Bartolomeo, of Giorgione. Also some of the younger artists of the *quattrocento* tradition were able to break away, partially at least, from the paths of their masters and join in the creation of the rebirth of antique art, the art of the High Renaissance. Notable in this category of men who worked in the styles of both centuries are Leonardo da Vinci and Andrea Sansovino.

Most active in the training of this new generation was Bertoldo di Giovanni, a bronze sculptor and a pupil of Donatello. In 1488, after the death of his wife, Clarice Orsini, Lorenzo the Magnificent gave over his villa near San Marco as a sort of academy where promising boys might draw from the antique and study sketches of the great masters under the tutelage of the aged Bertoldo. Amongst those who studied there, Vasari — in relating the story of Michelangelo's crushed nose — names Torrigiani, Rustici, Michelangelo, Granacci, Soggi, Bugiardini, Baccio da Monte Lupo, Lorenzo di Credi, and Andrea Contucci. The last two were twenty-nine and twenty-eight years old respectively, while Soggi at that time was only eight. We may suppose, then, that the instruction varied a great deal according to the attainments of the various pupils. Consequently, it now becomes necessary to determine the part played by Bertoldo in the education of Andrea Sansovino.

During these years, 1488–1491, Andrea was a practising sculptor; he was an independent artist of sufficient standing to gain admittance to the Arte in 1491. In other words, his technical training was complete, and he had established his ability as a sculptor. Bertoldo's contribution must have been in the way of criticism and theory. To make a deduction of the principles that Bertoldo may have taught, let us compare his sculpture with that of Pollajuolo. Both worked in bronze. Both were most skilful in composing single figures or small groups in the round. Both were fond of the nude and deeply interested in anatomy. Pollajuolo preferred a jagged, broken outline with the limbs projecting by themselves; he liked a violent display of taut muscles and agonizing emotions. He preferred to have the legs set far apart. Bertoldo liked a more closed outline with the limbs subtly disposed so as to build up a strong spiral rhythm. Movement is more apt to be centripetal than centrifugal. Oftentimes he uses an attitude of *contraposto*. He employed his knowledge of anatomy to achieve a feeling of absolute and inevitable harmony amongst the various parts rather than to express dramatic action. Such a coordination of the figure as Bertoldo sought required in him a working knowledge of anatomy, much as a poet must have a working mastery of words. Bertoldo was more interested in this "poem" of anatomy than in the graphic narration which was the aim of Pollajuolo.

Of course, one cannot say that all the differences which distinguish a work of Sansovino after his return from Portugal from an early work are due to Bertoldo's teaching. But within certain bounds, deductions of value can be made. Nearly all of these qualities tend toward the antique: more idealized heads which show little if any emotion; static poses, often with a slight *contraposto* and an S curve with one hip thrown out; and a more pronounced tendency to model in the round even if the figures are in relief.

From neither of these masters could Sansovino have learned to chisel the arabesque ornamentation he loved so dearly. Later,

Roman floral reliefs taught him, but already in the Corbinelli altar he was a master of this decoration. Nor from these masters did he gain his great ability to carve in marble, since neither Pollajuolo nor Bertoldo used that medium. On the other hand, it is exceedingly strange that we have no bronzes to attribute to Andrea. Vasari mentions the bronze railing of the Corbinelli chapel, but that is lost. One is tempted to suggest that certain bronze statuettes may come from his hand; for example, the *Hercules* in Berlin and the *David* formerly in the Morgan collection, both of which have been attributed to Antonio Pollajuolo.

The St. Lawrence Altar in Sta. Chiara at Monte San Savino

Whether this altar (Fig. 18) was done before or during Sansovino's study with Bertoldo is, of course, impossible to prove, but it does exhibit traces of his later style. Previous writers have been, I believe, too ready to characterize it as very early because of a certain awkwardness in its composition and in the proportions of some of the figures. The composition was a familiar Brunelleschi *motif*. The presence of the altar in the sculptor's native village gives credence to the theory that I am advancing, namely that the altar was made for some friend or group whom the artist felt obliged to accommodate, yet whose poverty prevented his spending much time upon the undertaking. The use of the inferior material — it was not even glazed — adds weight to the hypothesis that the patron was poor. In one sense only is the St. Lawrence altar a finished work; it was made to be set up as an altar, that is indisputable; in all other respects one should criticize it as one would a model or sketch. Clay was the material in terms of which most renaissance sculptors thought, in which they created models before translating their ideas into the more durable and more monumental materials of marble and bronze. And that Sansovino followed this general custom we may be sure from the character of his finished productions. In a sketch the artist may show personal peculiarities and abnormalities which do not appear in his more finished works.

Let us look at the altar itself (Fig. 18). In a central shell-headed niche stands St. Lawrence, wearing his deacon's garb and holding in his hands a book and a wooden grill which rests on the base of the niche. In similar niches on either side, and standing somewhat lower than St. Lawrence, who is on a low base, are statues of the two plague saints, Sebastian and Roch. In the lunette are two running angels holding a wreathed crown over St. Lawrence's head. A heavy frame decorated with bunches of fruit, balusters, and garlands surrounds the part already described. A predella below is so divided by similar balusters as to have two half-length bearded saints (Fig. 19) wearing monastic habits, in spaces corresponding to the width of the frame above, and between them three panels, likewise separated by balusters, with reliefs illustrating scenes from the lives of the saints over them. The panel on the left portrays the decapitation of St. Sebastian, the central relief depicts the martyrdom of St. Lawrence on a grill, and the third scene (Fig. 20) shows St. Roch visiting a victim of the plague.

Until recently the altar was not easy to study because the reredos was hidden under an annoying layer of paint and the predella was heavily whitewashed. As the consequence of an order issued by the Commissioner of Fine Arts, the local sacristan removed the paint and whitewash as best he could. The result is hardly an improvement: the paint-spotted clay — some of the pigment would not wash off — was unevenly baked, varies in color, and is difficult to photograph.

The altar is replete with direct influences from the sculpture of Donatello. This is not true of the works we have considered so far. Now Sansovino studied under Bertoldo, and Bertoldo was the pupil of Donatello and heir to his drawings and models. Is it not presumable, then, that we have here a piece from the years when Andrea frequented the Medici gardens? The architecture both in general design and in detail, the use of the fruit and vegetable frame decoration, and the *motif* of the running angels holding a crown — all these point to a date before the end of the fifteenth century. Since Sansovino probably left for Portugal in 1491 and did not return to Florence until 1500, it is likely that this work is before 1491.[25] The figure of St. Lawrence has more than a slight resemblance to Donatello's *St. Louis* and is even closer to the clay bust of *St. Leonard* in the sacristy of S. Lorenzo: Sansovino must have been studying those works of his great predecessor when he modeled this figure. At the same time there is a distinct relationship between this St. Lawrence and the *St. Anthony* of Jacopo Tatti, which is in S. Petronio at Bologna. Likewise does the St. Roch hark back to the *St. George* of the Or San Michele in its stance, in the relaxed arms, in the drapery falling behind the legs, and — most of all — in the querulous expression accompanied by a puckering of the brows, an expression that Sansovino will use again and again. What a contrast the St. Sebastian (Fig. 21) offers when compared with the torso of Christ on the Corbinelli *Pietà*! Gone is the detailed modeling of ribs and muscles inherited from Antonio Pollajuolo, the goldsmith, and come is the soft anatomical treatment of the *cinquecento* to be found in the Christ of the baptistry group, the Temperance of the Basso tomb, and the *Bacchus* of Andrea's pupil, Jacopo.[26]

An unsuspected ability to portray force and anguish in actions is discovered in the predella scenes. One regrets that Sansovino did not continue to develop this remarkable phase of his artistic powers. As in the predella panels of the Corbinelli altar, this quality goes back to the influence of Pollajuolo. The half-length figures of monks with long, stringy beards and knitted brows will reappear as God the Father in Sta. Maria del Popolo and as the high priest in the *Marriage of the Virgin* at Loreto, and be reincarnated dozens of times in the prolific school of which Andrea is the father in the sixteenth century.

I shall not enter into a study of the fruit garlands which decorate the frames of both the altars in Sta. Chiara. Such a study is important, but is so intricate in its relation to the ornament used by the della Robbia and other makers of terra-cotta altars that I leave that work to a specialist versed in such matters.

II

SANSOVINO IN PORTUGAL

Toward the close of the fifteenth century Portugal was one of the richest and most enterprising countries in Europe. More than fifty years of exploration in Africa culminated in 1488 when Bartholomeu Dias doubled the Cape of Good Hope, thus proving that India was accessible by sea. King John II (1481–1495) strengthened the power of the throne by the execution of eighty of his most puissant nobles. He negotiated the famous treaty of Tordesillas which gave to Portugal all the newly discovered lands east of 370 leagues west of Cape Verde. Indeed, by his sound reconstruction of the home government, and by his eager and liberal patronage of exploring and trading expeditions, John II prepared the way for the luxurious triumph of his successor, Emmanuel (1495–1515), the richest monarch that Europe had known since antiquity.

The name of Andrea becoming famous, the King of Portugal requested his services of Lorenzo the Magnificent, in whose garden, as was said, he studied drawing. Lorenzo sent him, and he did many works of sculpture and architecture for that king, particularly a splendid palace with four towers and many other edifices. A part of the palace was painted from cartoons by Andrea's hand. Andrea drew very well, as one can see in our book of designs, wherein there are some drawings by Andrea which are finished with the point of charcoal. We have besides in our possession certain architectural studies of great merit. For the same king, he also carved an altar in wood with figures of the prophets. Likewise he did a battle-piece in clay, which was to have been carved in marble, representing scenes of victories from the wars of that king over the Moors. Amongst all Andrea's works one can never see one more spirited or forceful than this, be it for the action and varied attitudes of the horses, for the carnage of the dead, or for the wild fury of the soldiers in deadly combat. He made also a figure of St. Mark in marble, a thing of rare beauty. Andrea likewise tried his hand at some difficult things of architecture according to the use of that country, in order to please the king. I saw a book of these which

his heirs had at Monte San Savino.   They say now that it is in the hands of
Master Girolamo Lombardi, who was his pupil, and, as I shall say later, to
whom certain works of Andrea were left for finishing.

When Andrea had been nine years in Portugal, he was tired of service
there, and desired to see once more his relatives and friends in Tuscany; and
since he had got together a fair sum of money, he determined, with the good
leave and favor of the king, to return to his own country. He got this permission from the king, but not without difficulty, and returned to Florence, leav-
ing behind him one who could complete his unfinished works.

Arrived in Florence, he began in 1500 a marble group of St. John baptizing
Christ.[1]

Thus Vasari in the second edition of his *Lives* (1568) sets the
stage for the study of Sansovino in Portugal. In his first edition
(1550) the Aretine biographer merely states that Andrea did
many works of architecture and sculpture in Portugal.[2] It seems
probable, then, that he learned further details of Sansovino's
sojourn abroad, during the period 1550–1568.

Since Vasari mentioned the book of drawings which he saw in
possession of the heirs at Monte San Savino, it would be well to
inquire when he might have been in that village. In 1537–1538
he was painting the large fresco which still exists in Sant' Agostino.[3] Through letters [4] from Vincenzo Borghini, the poet and
art critic, and from Cardinal Giovanni Maria del Monte, we learn
that Vasari went to Monte San Savino in 1548 and 1552. Once
he stopped there on his way from Arezzo to Rome and the other
time, or probably several times, he went at the request of his
friend the cardinal. The heirs mentioned are doubtless the
children of Andrea, who, it may be thought, furnished Vasari
with detailed and accurate information concerning their father's
activities in Portugal. On the other hand, if we consider that
Sansovino did not marry until 1516 when he was fifty-six years
old, only thirteen years before his death, it becomes clear that his
children would not have received much information directly from
their father, and that of a certainty they would not have remem-

bered it word for word some twenty years after his decease. It may be that letters and drawings from his sojourn in Portugal afforded them information which they passed on to Vasari. In any case, I believe that there is margin to doubt the Aretine's accuracy, especially in regard to the time of Sansovino's stay in Portugal, which, figuring from Vasari's own words, would be from 1491 to 1500.[5] Dr. Carl Frey[6] found in the *Spogli Strozziani* (a mine of information from documents, many of which are lost) the following notice, which I quote as Frey wrote it: "1493. Andrea di Niccolo scultore lauora figure di marmo per la chiesa di S. Giouanni. (Zum zweiten Male verzeichnet sub 1495/96.)"

There is no reason to think that Strozzi or Frey made errors in transcribing this notice. Moreover, it is clear from the document of April 28, 1502,[7] that the "figure di marmo" had nothing to do with the baptismal group which is now over Ghiberti's *Doors of Paradise*. The work referred to, then, is lost or completely unidentified. That there was another "Andrea di Niccolo scultore" is hard to believe. In one of the documents antedating this, that of Santo Spirito, which we assume to concern Sansovino, the artist is mentioned in precisely the same terms. Furthermore, there is added reason to believe that Andrea returned to Florence and stayed there for quite some time from the way entries are made in the last document we have that precedes his enigmatic trip to Portugal, the record of his matriculation into the guild of "maestri di pietre e legname."[8]

"Andrea di nicolo di domenico dal monte a sansovino
de' dare a di 13 di febraio 1490 [1491 by our calendar]
lire xxiiii per la sua matricola......................lire xxiiii
et per sua tassa dell' anno 1490–91–92–93 e 1494 ....lire iii
et per sua tassa dell' anno 1495 ....lire — soldi xii
et per la tassa dell' anno 1496–1497 ....lire i soldi iiii
et per l'anno 1498–99–1500. 1501–1502–1503 ....lire iii soldi xii

The *matricola* and the first entry of dues were written in the same handwriting, and apparently at the same time. The fact that he paid for four years in advance would suggest that he knew he was going away from Florence for about that period of time. If the notice quoted from Frey means that Andrea was in Florence from 1493 to early in 1496 — and it is difficult to understand how one could interpret it otherwise — we could then comprehend the single annual payment of the guild tax for 1495. That he paid for the two years 1496 and 1497 together suggests that he intended to be away for another period of at least two years. Then follows the payment from 1498 to 1503. How is this to be interpreted? Did Andrea pay six years in advance in 1498? That is possible, but is it not likely that the payment was made after his final return from abroad? No longer was he a novice seeking the favor of the guild and careful to keep his dues paid; he was the second greatest sculptor of Italy, a man whose membership did honor to the guild. The dues may have been paid, therefore, as late as 1503. In summary, it would seem that Andrea Sansovino went to Portugal in 1491 to work for John II, that from 1493 to early in 1496 he was back in Italy, and that he then spent four or five years in Portugal in the service of King Emmanuel. The total time spent abroad would be about six years.

Now we are in a better position to understand the answer to a perplexing question which has arisen: how was it possible that a *quattrocento* sculptor, Sansovino, the man who carved the Corbinelli altar, could spend nine years in Portugal and return to Tuscany fully equipped to design the very classic and very advanced statues on the baptistry of Florence and in the cathedral of Genoa? The answer is that he was in Italy during the years 1493–1496, and that he was in the main stream of new developments in Italy. It is possible, too, that he may have been in

Rome a part of this time with Pollajuolo. If so, the decided classic transformation in his art might be attributed to Rome.

Of the works in Portugal which Vasari mentions, not a trace has come to light, nor has there been published any monument which proves that Sansovino established a school in that country. Because of the controversy that has been raging in placid Lusitania over this matter, it seems best to review the literature on the works of Sansovino in Portugal.

The "palace with four towers" was long said to have been that palace on the present Praça do Comérico at Lisbon, which was destroyed in the earthquake of 1755. Haupt[9] at first believed this identification, which is not conclusively contradicted by old views of the city of Lisbon. Later, Haupt[10] decided from descriptions — he had not seen it — that the castle of Alvito in the Alemtejo answered Vasari's description.

He believed it had a square arcaded court, "something almost unheard of in Portugal [this is denied by Vasconcellos[11]], but almost the rule in Italy." As a matter of fact the court is not arcaded — there is only a row of rough plastered arches along one side; there are five and not four towers; there is no trace now of any fine painted decorations inside; and, in short, it is inconceivable that, even to please a king, an architect of the Italian Renaissance could ever have designed such a building.[12]

Joachim Rasteiro[13] thought that the villa of Bacalhoa em Azeitão, Ribatejo (Fig. 22), with its *three* towers and classic architecture, was a sounder attribution than Haupt's palace of Alvito, with its *five* towers and Moorish ornamentation. Beyond the presence of classic detail, the existence of towers, and the fact that the villa is a masterpiece — which I do not deny — Rasteiro has no cogent arguments. There is no proof, documentary or otherwise, that the present building was built by the Infanta D. Brites during Sansovino's stay in Portugal. Nor is it true that the architecture is Florentine, as Rasteiro asserts. Working with Rasteiro was the German ceramic authority, Theodor Rogge (the villa of Bacalhoa is justly famous for its tiles), who likewise published an article [14] attributing the villa to Andrea Sansovino. As proof for Sansovino's authorship he argues:

Dieses interessante Bauwerk, halb Stadtpalast, halb Villa, trägt mit seinem Loggien und Arkaden die unverfälschten edlen Formen italienischer Renaissance, wie ich sie in gleicher Weise an keinem andern in Portugal wahrgenommen. Ein Stück in dies Land verpflanzter florentinischer Kunst tritt uns hier durchaus unvermittelt entgegen. . . . Lediger die vier [*sic*] mit Kuppeln gedeckten Ecktürme, die zum Teil Treppenanlagen enthalten, sind als Zugeständnisse des Meisters an den "Gebrauch des Landes" zu betrachten und bilden einen Übergang dazu.

There are also some stairways with Gothic mouldings and pointed arches which would have to be explained away in the same fashion.

"Mit Sicherheit," continues Rogge, "ist anzunehmen, dass der Bau, wie er heute in seinen hauptsächlichsten Teilen mit Ausnahme der Ostfassade vor uns steht, durch D. Brites aufgeführt wurde, die Tochter des Infanten D. João und Gemahlin des Infanten D. Fernando." On the contrary, there is nothing certain about the date of the greater part of the building. The lintel over the main entrance, on the east façade — an integral part of the whole building — bears an inscription that it was made by Affonso de Albuquerque, who had purchased the property in December, 1528. The terra-cotta bust in a niche above this door is said to be a portrait of his son.

The loggia (Fig. 23) on the north side which seemed such pure Florentine work to Rasteiro and Rogge is hardly that. The date is well into the first half of the sixteenth century. Rasteiro suggested that the meritorious heads *in tondo* to be found in the spandrels of the lower arcade were portraits of the Infante D. João, master of the Order of Santiago, his wife, D. Izabel, the Infanta, D. Brites, and her husband, the Infante D. Fernando.

Perhaps so, but in any case their style dates them many years after the death of D. Brites in 1504.

Curiously enough, the villa still has an antique painted wooden ceiling, of which the photograph (Fig. 24) shows that part which is best preserved. Completely detached from the dwelling-house is a charming pavilion (Fig. 25), fronting a reservoir that is used for irrigation purposes. The style of its architecture, like that of all of the rest of the renaissance work on the villa, dates it well along in the sixteenth century.

In conclusion, it must be said that the four-towered palace of Sansovino has not yet been found, or at least not satisfactorily identified. All of the palaces for which claims have been advanced, with the exception of Bacalhoa, have little in common with Italian architecture about 1500, and nothing whatsoever of Sansovino's manner.

There exists some interesting literature dealing with the battle relief and the marble statue of St. Mark. Loureiro, director of the Academy of Lisbon, writing about 1840,[15] said that he had seen the marble St. Mark and the battle relief *in marble* before 1810 in the monastic church of S. Marcos de Tentugal near Coimbra. "Later," he adds, "when Massena invaded the Beira, they were much damaged, but one can still see something of them." Repeatedly efforts have been made to "see something of them," but with no success whatsoever. It is highly doubtful if Senhor Loureiro possessed the ability to judge if the works were by Sansovino, or even Italian, for that matter. The history of the church of San Marcos de Tentugal, the pantheon of the noble family, da Silva, is known from 1452 on, through its chronicles.[16] So far as is known, John II and Emmanuel had nothing to do with it. The high altar is by the French sculptor, Nicolas Chanterène, and the fifteenth- and sixteenth-century tombs are surely not by Italian sculptors. One learns from the chronicles that a statue of

St. Mark on an altar at the west end of the church was already missing in the seventeenth century. As before intimated, there is no reason to believe that this statue was that to which Vasari refers. Concerning the bas-relief of a battle scene, there is no further notice beyond the statement of Loureiro. Antonio Nibby [17] published a wooden relief of the *Siege of Arzilla* as the missing work of which Vasari spoke. This battle-piece went from the possession of the Duke of Altemps into the hands of the Roman jeweler, Castelani, who sold it to D. Fernando, the Prince-Consort of Queen Maria II of Portugal. Probably the relief is now in England in the estate of the late King Emmanuel. Until a photograph was published by Guido Battelli [18] it was necessary to accept Nibby's attribution. Now it is apparent that the existing relief is of much later date. Nor is this work in terracotta as Vasari says.

Of the altar carved in wood with figures of the prophets no trace remains, and there has been no attempt to identify it with any extant altar.

Signor Battelli published numerous monuments which he associated with Andrea's work in Portugal, but of these only one, a doorway in the sanctuary of Sto. Antonio da Castanheira,[19] might possibly be a work of one of his followers. It is a doorway with corbels within the upper corners, which is enframed by two arabesqued columns with Corinthian capitals bearing an architrave and cornice. The half-round columns are borne by plinths which are ornamented by reliefs of busts of a philosopher and a warrior. The two heads bear a distant resemblance to the terracotta head of Galba in Arezzo, and the peculiar use of the corbels may be derived from Sansovino, who, like his master, Pollajuolo, was fond of their use. The arabesques of both vegetable and animal *motifs* appear to be considerably later than 1500.

The architecture in Tomar which Battelli [20] would attribute to Sansovino, that is to say the chapel of N.S. da Conceição and the corridor of Celas in the convent of Tomar, are not even distantly related to his style. Senhor Teixeira [21] and Dr. Correia [22] have found good evidence for attributing them to João de Castilho.

In his old age, Joachim de Vasconcellos [23] stated that he had collected much material relating to Andrea Sansovino and his school in Portugal. When pressed to give evidence [24] he referred to the fireplace from Almeirim in the palace of Sintra, Graça, reliefs in the museum of Evora, the Quinta da 'Agua de Peixes, Bacalhoa, Vila Viçosa, Portalegre, and the Museum of Antique Art in Lisbon. I have visited all of these places which he mentions except the Quinta da 'Agua de Peixes and the town of Portalegre. The former is a country palace of the late fifteenth century with architectural detail of Moorish derivation, and its relationship with Sansovino, judging from photographs, could be assumed only if documents were forthcoming. The renaissance works in Portalegre of which I have seen photographs are of a date later than 1520 and similar in style to architectural sculpture of that period elsewhere in Portugal.

If there exists in Portugal any architecture by Andrea Sansovino it is probably in that "extravagant and difficult" style, the Emmanueline. In the absence of documents it would be folly to attribute any such architecture to his design.

I did, however, find one statue in Portugal that may have something to do with Sansovino. I refer to a painted terra-cotta statue of *St. Jerome* (Fig. 26) in a chapel of the transept of the monastic church of Belem on the outskirts of Lisbon. The saint is portrayed standing, half naked, gazing ecstatically at a cross which is supported by a tree trunk beside him, on which his left hand rests. He beats his bare chest with a stone in his right hand. The lion, quite small, is seated behind the saint's left leg. The bald head and short beard are rather unusual. The fixed eyes,

and the mouth opened in ecstasy, recall the St. James of the
Corbinelli altar. The treatment of the brow, the shape of the
nose, the strained tendons of the neck, the position of the arm,
the general stance, and the arrangement of the rough garment
are similar to the Genoa *Baptist*. Although the details of the
Baptist are more carefully finished, the anatomy is almost the
same in the two figures. More adequate photographs are necessary in order to determine the definite relationship of this figure
to the works of Sansovino.[25]

A lost drawing for the tomb of King John II was mentioned
about 1700 by Sebastiano Resta [26] in a letter to Giuseppe Ghezzi.
Resta wrote that this design for an architectural monument was
from the hand of Sansovino the Elder.

Vasari once speaks of Sansovino as having worked in Portugal
and Spain. It is possible that he may have been the "Andrés
florentín" mentioned in the documents of the cathedral of Toledo,
and extracted as follows: "En 15 de julio de 1500 se pagó á Andrés
florentín, la imagen de San Martín, que hizo por muestra del re-
tablo y por ir y venir á Benevente, con 3,750 maravedis." [27] Of interest in connection with this mention is the tomb of the great
cardinal, Don Pedro de Mendoza, in the *capilla mayor* of the
cathedral of Toledo. This monument, begun in 1494, has often
been associated with Sansovino's name.[28] No one has ever suggested that he designed or executed the sculpture of it. Only
the design for the architecture has been attributed to him. The
verification of this attribution is most difficult: the style is not
unlike his, as a comparison with the Corbinelli altar and the
drawings for the tombs of the Popolo shows, yet, with the exception of the little finial scrolls and the balusters between them, it
might well be the work of one of a large number of Italian artists
of that time. If Sansovino made drawings for the Mendoza
tomb, the carvers did not adhere to them closely.

III

SANSOVINO'S MATURITY IN FLORENCE

Sansovino may have returned to Florence from Portugal by
1501, for in August of that year Michelangelo was given the
commission of the great marble *David*, and Vasari [1] states that
Pietro Soderini had frequently proposed to give the block of
marble (out of which Agostino di Duccio had begun to carve a
prophet forty years earlier) to Leonardo da Vinci, then to Andrea
Contucci. [2] During these early years of the sixteenth century
Andrea Sansovino played no mean part in the formation of the
art of the High Renaissance, even when one considers that his
rivals in the creation of the new style were the giants of modern
art, Michelangelo, Leonardo, and Raphael. After the troublous
years of the French invasion, the dominance of Savonarola, and
the consequent anarchy, Florence was again the focus of the
greatest artistic activity in Europe. Florence was Florence once
more!

Sansovino took part in the fraternal gatherings of artists
which were characteristic of *cinquecento* Florence. Vasari gives
one notice in this regard, [3] which I quote. In the workshop of
Baccio d'Agnolo, "where many citizens and the foremost artists
assembled, especially in winter, remarkable discussions and many
disputes took place. The principal figure at these reunions was
Raphael, then a young man, and after him came Andrea Sansovino, Filippino, Majano, Cronaca, Antonio and Giuliano San
Gallo, Granaccio, and on rare occasions, Michelangelo."

Andrea remained in Florence until 1505, for on December 30,
1504, he accepted a commission to execute a marble tabernacle
for the high altar of the cathedral. [4] On January 18, 1505, he

received forty-two florins for a wooden model of the above tabernacle. On the last day of January the Arte di Lana was after him to finish the baptistry group;[5] and on the same day he rented a house in the parish of Santa Maria in Campo for three years from Maddalena, wife of Matteo Puccini.[6]

One might expect that after a long period of disruption Florence would have lost her supremacy in the arts. That was not so. The glory of her sons' achievements was spread abroad and loudly proclaimed by the foreign invaders. Orders for paintings, for statues, poured in from all Italy, from France, from Spain, from England, from Hungary. Local burghers individually, and collectively under the Arti, gave generous commissions. Even the weak, corrupt government patronized the artists. During these first five years of the *cinquecento* the greatest artists of Italy gathered in the city of Dante and Giotto. Leonardo, Michelangelo, Raphael, Fra Bartolomeo, Perugino, Filippino, all these and hundreds of lesser men, apprentices and skilled workers in the minor arts, were there. The city was a factory of art, and remained such until Julius II, Leo X, and King Francis spent fabulous sums to draw the artists to Rome or to France.

Naturally, this is the period of greatest development in Andrea Sansovino's life. He was in his forties, in full possession of his artistic powers, and he did not fail to benefit by the intensely critical atmosphere in which he was living.

The Terra-Cotta Madonna and Child in the Bargello

That this small group (Fig. 27) dates in the period after Sansovino's final return from Portugal is likely. It is true that there are certain resemblances to the Christ Child and the figures of the Virgin from the Corbinelli altar, but these resemblances are not so strong as its kinship to the Genoa *Madonna*, or, for that matter, to the *tondo* representation of the Virgin and Child on the Sforza tomb. The facial expressions, which in the St. Lawrence altar were pensive, have now become passionately emotional. The emotional distress of the Child, apparent in His face and in His body, turned in a rebellious attitude of *contraposto*, is met by the static placidity of the Virgin's body and the expression of profound understanding on her face. Such penetrating analysis of the deep emotional sympathy of the Mother and Son is not to be found in the artist's work which dates before his final return to Italy, and never does Sansovino achieve a greater success in this field. The lack of a more classical coiffure such as occurs on the *Madonna* at Genoa should not be held against my claim for the date of this work, since the Virgins of the *tondo* reliefs in Sta. Maria del Popolo lack it also, as do the Virtues of the baptismal font in Volterra.

The Baptismal Group of San Giovanni

The likelihood that Sansovino had earlier worked for the baptistry is fortified by a document of April 28, 1502,[7] that records the proposal which Andrea made to the Arte di Lana to replace the medieval group over the south door of the baptistry ("they are so stupid, that for a temple of the quality of the said church of San Giovanni it seems a downright shame that they are visible and that they remain there. Also they are so corroded that parts have already begun to fall, and what remains is toppling") with "la figura di Nostro Signore e quella di San Giovanni Batista, quando si battezzorono, di marmo." (Fig. 28.) I have given the last quotation in the Italian of the document to emphasize the clarity of the description of the group. Observe that it contains no mention of an accompanying angel, although the group to be replaced included one, and in time an angel was added to Sansovino's two figures, as we shall see later. The proposal was accepted, and Sansovino set to work in earnest, but some difficulties must have arisen, because, although he found time to complete commissions for Volterra and Genoa in the meanwhile, the group was left unfinished when he went to Rome in 1505. Indeed, on the 25th of January, 1505, we learn from a document published by Milanesi with the one mentioned above that the figures were not yet finished and that the Arte charged him to have them done in ten months. But Pope Julius called Andrea to Rome.

The next mention of the group is perhaps in a notice which Frey[8] culled from the *Spogli Strozziani*. Under the date of January 27, 1511, we read as follows: "figure di marmo, che sono nell' Opera di Sta. Maria del Fiore, si conduchino in quella di S. Giovanni." Then follows in 1514 the monochromatic painting of the group by Andrea del Sarto in the Chiostro dello Scalzo. The painter may have worked from clay models rather than the unfinished marbles, so that one cannot use the fresco as evidence for the state of finish of the marbles at that time. Interesting in connection with this fresco of the Scalzo is Vasari's statement that Jacopo Sansovino often made models for his friend, Andrea del Sarto.[9] In the first edition of the *Lives* (1550) Vasari says that Sansovino did not finish the group, and in the second edition (1668) he adds, "The things left unfinished at Florence are still in the Opera di San Giovanni." Our next testimony comes from 1584, the date of the only edition of Raffaello Borghini's *Il Riposo* which was published during the lifetime of the author. In his charming dialectical method Borghini discussed the statues as follows: "But who began the two statues over the doorway of San Giovanni, where Christ is baptized by St. John? They seem very fine to me. They were made by Andrea of Monte a Sansovino — replied Sirigatto — but because he did not completely finish them, Vincenzio Danti the Perugian completed them, as

you know. And they are worthy of notice, as you can see." [10]
Later on [11] in speaking of Danti, Borghini says, "He finished in
Florence the two statues of marble which stand over the doorway
of San Giovanni, which Andrea of Monti a Sansovino had left
incomplete." We learn then from Borghini that Vincenzo Danti
finished the two statues of Sansovino between 1568 (Vasari's
second edition) and 1584, that the group was placed above
Ghiberti's *Doors of Paradise* (this is clear from the context), and
that the group consisted of two figures only. During the course
of the next century a third figure appeared, as the following
quotation [12] demonstrates: "Over the architrave of this door the
three marble statues of Christ baptized by St. John the Baptist
are in part by Andrea dal Monte a S. Sovino, and in part by the
aforementioned Vincenzo Danti da Perugia." Then we are
informed [13] that the third figure is an angel made of clay, that he
holds a towel to dry our Lord, and that *all three* are the work of
Andrea da Monte Sansovino, set up in 1502! Ultimately we
read [14] that the angel of clay has been removed, that it was the
work of neither Sansovino nor Danti but of a far inferior hand of
a much later time, and that this was the judgment of no less a
person than Signor Innocenzio Spinazzi, "excellent sculptor,"
who at that very time was engaged upon the task of replacing
it with the praiseworthy angel of marble which today stands
beside Christ and the Baptist above the *Doors of Paradise*
(Fig. 29).

More than any other production of Sansovino's maturity
has this group been praised, praised even by critics so seeped in
the undeniably excellent, but very different, qualities of early
renaissance art that they make the pronouncement of "empty
classicism" on all truly sixteenth-century art (Michelangelo
excepted, of course). Jakob Burckhardt, one of the sanest and
most penetrating critics of Italian art, spoke in the following

tones of this work:[15] "What nobility in the figure of Christ! and what devoutness in expression and gesture! In the Baptist one rediscovers a more powerful expression of that grandiose motive of strong suppressed emotion used by Ghiberti on a relief of the north door." He was right, too, in tracing the inspiration of the work back to Ghiberti. Bode in the fifth edition of the *Cicerone* [16] admits that the group not only presents a high degree of beauty in the figures, but is a work of true grandeur, and of monumental conception.

A comparison which Wölfflin [17] makes is so interesting that I must quote it in its entirety:

Let us compare A. Sansovino's group on the baptistery with Verrocchio's *Baptism*. The former gives a perfectly novel rendering of the theme. The Baptist is not advancing, he stands calmly in his place. His breast is turned towards the spectator, not towards Christ. The head alone, boldly facing sideways, follows the direction of the hand, which holds the bowl of water at arm's length over the Redeemer's head. There is no anxious following after Jesus, no straining forward of the body. The Baptist, calm and reticent, performs the ceremony, a symbolic action, which does not depend for its efficacy on any precise method of execution. Verrocchio's John is bending over like an apothecary pouring a draft into a bottle, and full of anxiety lest a drop should be wasted. His eye follows the water; in Sansovino's group it rests on the face of Christ. The figure of Christ is likewise changed. He is represented as a ruler, not as a poor teacher. Verrocchio depicts him standing unsteadily in the river, the water swirling round his shrunken legs. A later age gradually dispensed with the standing in the water, unwilling to sacrifice the clear representation of the figure to commonplace realism, but the pose itself became easy and dignified. Sansovino's attitude is graceful and buoyant; the leg on which no weight is thrown is thrust out to the side. There is a beautiful continuous line in place of the angular jagged movement. The shoulders are squared, the head only being slightly sunk. The arms are crossed over the breast, the natural development of the conventional motive of the hands clasped in prayer.[18] This is the grand gesture of the sixteenth century.

One wonders what parts of the two figures were worked on by Vincenzo Danti. It would seem that the Baptist was finished by Andrea, and that the later sculptor's chisel was confined to completing certain parts of the figure of Christ. The work diverging most from the practice of Sansovino is the treatment of the supporting trees, the knees, and the musculature of the calves. The torso, arms, and head of Jesus are precisely what one would expect of Sansovino at this stage of his development. The beard does show a lack of detail which is not compatible with Andrea's work of this time. A close examination of a recent photograph (Fig. 28), however, leads one to believe that this apparent breadth of handling is due to the erosive action of rain water, and that originally the beard was indicated by the same wavy lines that are used in the locks of hair which fall on the shoulders of Christ.

Another question to which a final answer cannot be given follows: Was Sansovino responsible for the tabernacle (Fig. 29) with two columns that partially enframes this group and the angel? I proved above that there exists no basis for supposing that Sansovino intended the group to consist of three figures, yet the design of this bit of architecture is in the style of the early sixteenth century, and furthermore, Rustici, only a few years later (in 1506), not only took on the commission to execute a group of *three* figures of the *Preaching of the Baptist* to go above the north door, but also designed the architectural enframement. The pinched proportions of the architrave and the unstructural handling of the volutes of the capitals are not out of keeping with Sansovino's ideas of architectural design.[19] Yet why would he project such an inadequate tabernacle if he intended the group to consist of two statues only?

The Baptismal Font at Volterra

On June 9, 1502, the commune of Volterra gave to "magistro Andrea de monte Sancti Sabini" the commission for a marble baptismal font to cost thirty florins. It is octagonal (Fig. 30), with seated figures of four Virtues and a relief of the Baptism of Christ on the five exposed sides, and bears the inscription "A NATIVITATE HIESU FILII DEI ANNO MDII". One learns [20] that it stood neglected in a storeroom until 1828, when it was placed in its present location, a niche of the ancient baptistry, and that a little statue of St. John was removed from it (the figure in question must have been part of the cover) in 1772 to decorate a holy water font of the cathedral. There is no later mention of the little statue of St. John, which is now lost.

The work is simple, and commonplace in architectural design. It is obviously in Sansovino's style, yet it is so dull that the critics who have seen it have pronounced it unhesitatingly a work of his shop. The mouldings and palmettes in the spandrels of the niches are uninspired adaptions from the Corbinelli altar. The Virtues (Fig. 31), however, are not without merit, as can be seen when they are photographed from an advantageous point of view, a thing difficult to accomplish because of improper lighting and the enfolding walls of the niche in which the font is set. Indeed, two of these reliefs are next to impossible to see, and one wonders if three whole sides may not be embedded in the baptistry wall! The fragile bodies of Christ and John in the relief of the baptism are in striking contrast to the robust athletes above Ghiberti's doors. Standing in the Jordan, which issues from a rocky defile, Christ is represented humbly and piously bending over while the Baptist pours the water on His head. Is it not possible that this is an adaption of a preliminary study for the Florentine group? It is of interest to note in this connection that the scene includes no angel.

The Genoa Statues of the Madonna and St. John the Baptist

Of the same new style as the group for the baptistry of Florence are two statues, a *Madonna* and a *St. John the Baptist*, which Sansovino did for the cathedral of Genoa. The statues were made in Florence, as one learns from Gaye,[21] who published a permit of the Dieci di Balia giving Andrea permission to ship the statues through Pisan territory on their way to Genoa. The date of the permit was January 13, 1504. Working on the assumption that the sculptor spent some time in Genoa, Santi Varno[22] found enough specious attributions to fabricate quite an extensive "Genoese Period" for our artist. As a matter of fact, there is no proof that Sansovino remained in Genoa any length of time.

Matteo Civitale had made six statues of illustrious forbears of the Baptist to decorate all but two of the niches in the chapel in which are enshrined the ashes of the Precursor. Thus the size and location of the two new figures were conditions dictated to Sansovino. The chapel opens full width (*circa* 30 feet) off the left aisle of San Lorenzo. On either side are three niches containing Civitale's statues of *Adam, Eve, Habakkuk, Isaiah, Elizabeth,* and *Zacharias*; then the chapel narrows about six feet on both sides, and it is on these walls, parallel to the main axis of the church, that one finds the two statues which most interest us. As one can see from the photographs (Figs. 32 and 33), the attention of all three of Sansovino's figures — including the Child — is definitely focused. The object of their interest is the shrine of the Baptist, which is between the two niches in a small choir. The lighting of the statues is bad, because they are in comparatively dark corners and the well-lighted choir between them causes a certain contraction of the pupils in the spectators' eyes. Women who are interested in the sculpture of the chapel must be content to view it from a distance, for the sex suffers exclusion from the Baptist's chapel to atone for the iniquity of Salome.

The *John* here (Fig. 32) is the same as he of the baptistry in Florence, with slight changes in posture, clothing, and refinement to meet the new requirements of a single figure in an interior

niche. Because the work was protected from the weather the
drapery is more involved and the surfaces of flesh and stuffs are
more finished. Veins, tendons, bones, and muscles are carved
with striking realism, and one wonders if the *Baptist* of Florence
has not weathered more than is generally realized. The fleece of
the undergarment, the beard, and the hair — which is braided
back in a curious fashion over the nape of the neck — are arranged in disorder with the greatest care. Truly this is work of
the sixteenth century! The perfection of anatomy here exhibited
recalls contemporaneous achievements of Leonardo and Michelangelo. The scientific delineation of muscles, veins, and the
underlying bone structure, however, is one more indication that
Sansovino was a true pupil of Pollajuolo. It is of interest to note
that the Baptist is represented with a fuller beard than he had
in the later fifteenth century.

The *Mary and Child* (Fig. 33) is the intermediate example of
Sansovino's three great creations of this group — the others
being the terra-cotta of the Bargello and that with St. Anne in
Sant' Agostino in Rome. It is surprising to find how diverse the
types of the Madonna are, and how the face of the Child varies
to maintain a family resemblance to His Mother. The artist
must have made an intensive study of the physiognomical rela-
tionships between mothers and their offspring. The complete
harmony of mood of the Madonna and her Son is a contributing
factor to the unity of the group. The most classic note of this
work is the treatment of Mary's hair in a series of undulating
strands flowing from a part down the middle of her head. It
needs to be stated, since there is a wide discrepancy from the
truth amongst the ranks of casual commentators on Sansovino
in this regard, that these figures show no further signs of copying
the antique. The drapery is totally different from any known in
ancient art; its ancestry is, indeed, to be found in Gothic sculp-

ture. The features are idealized, but one would be hard put to find antique models. Furthermore, the canon of proportions is six heads, rather an unusual canon for a close imitator of the classic!

Both statues are signed on the base: "SANSVVINVS FLORENINVS FACIEBAT." In these statues and the *Baptist* at Florence one sees for the first time good examples of Andrea Sansovino's new grand manner of handling drapery, a style of treatment which much influenced his followers.

Both of these figures served as inspirations for productions of the Aprile-Gaggini shop in Genoa. There is a free copy of the *Madonna and Child* in the Cartuja at Seville, and a reduced version of the *Baptist* on one of the Ribera tombs in the University church of the same city.

The St. Anthony Abbot in Lucca

"He (Filippino Lippi) also did some things at Lucca, notably a panel in a chapel of the church of San Ponziano of the friars at Monte Oliveto, in the middle of which is a fine *St. Andrew*, standing in a niche, by that great sculptor, Andrea Sansovino." [23]

This "*St. Andrew*" is, I believe, a painted wooden statue of *St. Anthony Abbot* (Fig. 34) which stands in a niche off the choir of the church of Sant' Andrea in Lucca. Fabriczy [24] attributed this carving to Baccio da Monte Lupo, but a brief study of the matter is sufficient to prove his attribution untenable. On the other hand, this majestic *St. Anthony* — it is really under life-size — bears a close resemblance to the Baptists of Sansovino. The general formation of the head (Fig. 35), the contraction of the brow, the treatment of the hair and beard, and above all the feeling of tensity, conform with Sansovino's work of this period. There is even a similarity between this head and that of the St. Matthew on the Corbinelli altar (Fig. 36). Furthermore, the cusped formation of the bunch of drapery beside the book over *St. Anthony's* left hip is almost a Sansovino signature (cf. the similar nodule of drapery over the left hip of the Genoa *Baptist*, that under the left hand of the *Madonna* at Genoa, the treatment of edges of the drapery of the angels and the folds around the waist of the St. Agatha of the Madonna altar in Monte San Savino, and the cloud formation in many of Andrea's reliefs, notably the *Annunciation* at Loreto).

The *St. Anthony* is one of the noblest of Sansovino's creations. Hitherto the old hermit had been a doddering, senile septuaginary, leading a ridiculous rat-like pig. Here the pig's head, the fine modeling of which accords with Sansovino's skilful depiction of animals, appears beside the saint's left foot; it is treated quite properly as the symbol of vanquished gluttony and relegated to a subordinate position. The bell for exorcising demons, too, is not conspicuous, and it is conceivable that Vasari may not have noticed these attributes in the dark church. Surely the monumentality of this vigorous old man would befit a representation of the warrior, St. Andrew.

IV

SANSOVINO IN ROME

FOLLOWING his brief triumph in the High Renaissance of Florence, comes a greater glory for Sansovino in the Eternal City. For glorious his work was, although seen in the perspective of today it was modest in comparison with the heroic accomplishments of Michelangelo and Raphael.

Julius II had been pope for almost two years when in 1505 he called Andrea Sansovino to Rome. Doubtless the sculptor owed this patronage to his mentor, Giuliano da San Gallo, who was a personal friend of the Rovere and had even accompanied him into exile in France. On the other hand, it is possible that the pope knew Andrea through Pollajuolo, who had been the creator of the tomb of the pope's uncle, Sixtus IV.

Never was there a pope who loved art as did Giuliano della Rovere. And never had there been a pope who was more capable of organizing and realizing great projects, artistic as well as military. Nicholas V (1447–1455) had dreamed of building a new Rome, but the time was not ripe, and his dream remained only a dream. Sixtus IV (1471–1484) had the energy and the will to create a Rome that would have been worthy of the primate of Christendom. But money was lacking. So it is not surprising to find Julius II putting his state in order economically, because he knew that his treasury must be great if his dreams were to come true. And he did this in spite of costly wars.

The Rome of 1503 was a very different city from the Rome of today, or from the Rome of Constantine. In 1503 it was very small. Although it was defended by the Aurelian walls the inhabited part occupied but a minor portion of the area within

the imperial circuit. The heart of the city was the region around
the Piazza Navona. In general the habitations were close to
their water supplies, the Tiber and — for a very few people — the
trickle of water brought by the Acqua Vergine to the Trevi
fountain. Because of the lack of water the hills were uninhabited
except for the Capitoline and a few houses on the Quirinal near
the Trevi fountain. The Coelian and the Aventine slept in the
profoundest solitude of grassy ruins amidst groves and orchards.
The Viminal and the Esquiline supported vineyards and gardens
where the soil was not too choked by debris. The mastodonic
walls of the great imperial baths of Diocletian, Caracalla, and
Constantine stood out boldly in their rural settings. The Forum
was a cow pasture. And the pilgrim, come to the Eternal City,
had to walk through miles of country lanes to make the required
round of the great basilicas.

With the exception of the Corso, then still known as the Via
Lata, the streets were crooked; they were often so narrow that a
horse could barely pass through them. Streets and squares were
cleaned only on the days when the pope must pass that way.
Low houses, often of wood, with exterior staircases, darkened
the narrow streets with their overhanging balconies. Each street
had a character all its own. When the muddy red Tiber swept
over the Campus Martius to a depth of several feet, which it did
frequently, the plight of the Romans must have been miserable
indeed.

Yet Rome was the bright star of Europe. It had over fifty
basilicas, some ruinous, to be sure, but they were filled with
ancient mosaics and sarcophagi as well as paintings and sculpture
by Italy's greatest artists from Giotto and Cavallini to Pollajuolo
and Pintoricchio. Dozens of *campanili* gave interest to the
Roman skyline. The medieval Capitol with its lofty belfry and
the Aracoeli's façade of gleaming mosaic must have been a

splendid sight. Old St. Peters was the richest museum in the
world, with the finest works of Christian art of all periods. For
the artist, Rome had antique sculpture to show in its *Marcus
Aurelius* at the Lateran, its *Horse Tamers* on the Quirinal, its
columns of Trajan and Marcus Aurelius, and many works in the
palaces of wealthy merchants and prelates. The *Apollo Belvedere*,
destined to be worshipped as the *summum bonum* of beauty for
three centuries, was in the personal collection of Giuliano della
Rovere. The election of Giuliano marked a decided increase in
the mad rush to collect antiques. Farms were dug over, the bed
of the Tiber searched, agents were sent to Greece and the Near
East. Fakes abounded, prices were fabulous. This feverish
activity brought immediate results: on January 14, 1506, the
Laocoon, on May 19, 1507, the *Torso Belvedere*, and in 1512 the
Ariadne and the *Tiber* came to light. All of these were placed in
the Belvedere, along with two ancient sarcophagi. Already
Innocent VIII had begun a museum on the Capitoline.

A traveler coming from the north on the Via Flaminia entered
Rome through the Porta del Popolo, a city gate of no distinction. Just within lay a sordid open space where one now finds the
spacious piazza. For the most part it was bordered by stone walls
and a few poor huts, but beyond extended a view of the Aracoeli
seen through the Arco di Portogallo down the delightfully straight
Via Lata. Close at the left of the city gate at the foot of the
Pincio lay the Augustinian church of Sta. Maria del Popolo, in
whose adjacent convent (destroyed in the sack of Rome, 1527)
the popes made their first halts when returning from the north.
There distinguished guests were hospiced before they made official entries into the papal capital. And it was the custom for
them to leave a ducat at the altar on their arrival.

Early in the twelfth century the neighborhood of the Pincio
was freed from the evil spirits which haunted the locality of

Nero's tomb. Pope Pascal II with his own hands felled an especially malignant walnut tree, and supervised the throwing of Nero's ashes into the Tiber. The people rejoiced, and in their gratitude built a chapel which became known as Santa Maria del Popolo. Why the della Rovere family chose this obscure, suburban church as its favorite sanctuary is a mystery, especially when one considers that both Francesco and Giuliano della Rovere held their cardinalships over S. Pietro in Vincoli, that SS. Apostoli was almost a part of their family palace, and that both Giuliano and his uncle had begun their ecclesiastical careers in Franciscan garb. The importance of the church dates from the time (1472–1477) when it was rebuilt by Sixtus IV. Perhaps the upstart family wanted a sanctuary which was its own almost from the beginning. Sixtus loved to make his devotions there, and there to celebrate with pomp the important events of his reign. Sta. Maria del Popolo soon became not only the pantheon of the Rovere family but also a favorite burial place for cardinals. Its wealth of renaissance tombs is unsurpassed.[1]

The Tombs in Santa Maria del Popolo

As we have seen above, at the beginning of the year 1505 Andrea had taken a house in Florence for three years, and had begun a tabernacle of the host for Santa Maria del Fiore. It is neither in keeping with what we know of the artist's character nor compatible with the offers of later commissions from the cathedral to suppose that Andrea broke his Florentine contracts and went to Rome on his own account. There must have been a papal order, and this brings us to the conclusion that Sansovino's sepulchre of Cardinal Ascanio Sforza was built at the expense of his lifelong enemy and successful rival for the tiara, Giuliano della Rovere. An inscription on the tomb corroborates this magnanimous gesture, which is indicative of Giuliano's nature in its generosity, ostentation, and courage. Sansovino was attached to the papal court with the position of "controllore della Basilica di San Pietro." [2]

Ascanio Sforza, son of Francesco Sforza and brother of Galeazzo Maria and Lodovico il Moro, became a cardinal in 1484 and enjoyed great success in diplomatic intrigue on behalf of Innocent VIII, who rewarded him liberally with rich benefices. In 1492, at the conclave which elected Alexander VI, his chances for obtaining the tiara were very high, but to preclude the election of Giuliano della Rovere he threw his support to the Borgia. Yet in spite of this he lived an uncertain and troubled life during the pontificate of Alexander, and was, we may be sure, marked for death by the Borgias after Milan fell. At the battle of Rivalla in 1500 the Venetians took him prisoner and turned him over to the French, who kept him incarcerated for several years at Bourges. He was permitted to return to the conclave which elected Julius II, but died soon afterward (May 28, 1505), probably in Rome, of the plague, although there were not wanting those who thought he had been poisoned. All his life he had been a bitter and resourceful foe of Giuliano della Rovere.

This tomb (Fig. 37) is but a part of a project for the rebuilding and enlarging of the whole east end of the church.[3] Bramante was probably the architect in charge, Guillaume de Marcillat and Claude de Marseilles made the fine windows, Pinturicchio painted the choir ceiling, and Andrea Sansovino built the tomb of Ascanio in the north wall of the choir. It is absurd to imagine that the tomb of Girolamo Basso was not projected at the same time as a necessary component of the design. Tombs were often made long before their future owners were ready to occupy them.

It has been suggested that Bramante may have designed the architecture of the tomb,[4] but this opinion is, I believe, wholly unwarranted. The monument (Fig. 37) is an elaboration of the *quattrocento* wall tomb, the chief addition being the rounded, smaller side niches which make it resemble an antique triumphal arch, a *motif* that Sansovino had employed several years before in the Santo Spirito altar. These niches contain figures of the Virtues Justice and Prudence, and above them are the seated Virtues Faith and Hope, which serve to make the transition to the higher central cornice that is surmounted by two candelabra bearing angels flanking a figure of God the Father seated over a shell and scroll device with the arms of the pope. Is it possible that Sansovino was familiar with the Venetian ducal tombs designed by Pietro Lombardi some thirty years previously?[5] In a general way the Venetian tombs are similar to Sansovino's (more similar than was the tomb of Paul II), with large central niches and smaller side niches containing statues of the Virtues, but they lack the definite and logical architectural system, composed of semi-columns with a complete entablature running right across, which is the governing idea of Sansovino's tombs. Architecture and sculpture are kept in complete interdependence, with the result that the organic unity of the monument as a whole is very marked.

The most startling and influential innovation, as well as that which has aroused most criticism, is the position of the sculptured figure of the cardinal. The real change from the earlier mode of representing the deceased is to be attributed to the new philosophy of life and attitude toward death, rather than to a whim of the artist. The fifteenth-century sculptor depicted the cadaver of the deceased stretched out on a rich triumphal bier; here the cardinal is asleep, or rather resting (well did Ascanio deserve that rest)! It is a posture that had been widely accepted for centuries. One need only look at pictures and reliefs of the Resurrection to discover figures in this conventional posture. In the fifteenth century the attitude was frequently used in a decorative way for the richness of its outline and the interesting disposition of the limbs.[6] The popularity of the reclining figure was heightened by Giuliano's purchase of the *Sleeping Ariadne* of the Vatican a few years later.

There are two main sources which may have influenced Sansovino's adoption of this *motif* for the effigy. The first and most obvious is the similar usage of the Etruscans and Romans. The second, which I have never heard advanced, is the medieval prototype to be found in England [7] and Spain.[8] A third explanation is the functional: the features of the deceased could be seen easily without tilting the funeral couch at an angle as did Desiderio in the Marsuppini tomb (this angle becomes distasteful when increased too much, as it was in some Roman tombs); and furthermore, the width of the central niche could be narrowed while still retaining the life-size portrait of the defunct.

J. A. Symonds[9] gives an amusing condemnation of the

evil custom of aping life and movement on the monuments of dead men which began to obtain when the motives of pure repose had been exhausted. "Why," asks the Duchess of Malfi, "do we grow fantastical in our death-bed? Do we affect fashion in the grave?" "Most ambitiously," answers Bosola. "Princes' images on their tombs do not lie as they were wont, seeming to pray up to heaven, but with their hands under their cheeks as if they died of the tooth-ache. They are not carved with their eyes fixed upon the stars, but as their minds were wholly bent upon the world, the selfsame way they seem to turn their faces." [10] A more trenchant criticism than this could hardly have been pronounced upon Andrea Contucci di Monte Sansovino's tombs of Ascanio Sforza and Girolamo della Rovere, if Bosola had been standing before them.

Nevertheless, Webster (or rather the source material from which he drew) had no very bad opinion of Sansovino's work, for in the same play [11] he has a pilgrim saying, "I have not seen a goodlier shrine than this; yet I have visited many," when standing before the Santa Casa (Fig. 49) at Loreto.

One can judge neither the value of the architectural *ensemble* nor the effect of individual statues from commercial photographs, such as Figure 37, which are taken so as to resemble elevations as much as possible. One must photograph these monuments from the point of view of the spectator to get the proper effect (Fig. 38), and one must take into account the vertical perspective, just as — we may be sure — the artist did.

It has been said that these tombs are poorly designed because the Virtues attract one's attention quite as much as the images of the prelates. But are not a man's virtues quite as important as his appearance? In any case, the Justice (Fig. 39) is widely accepted as the masterpiece of Cardinal Sforza's sepulchre. Whether or not the Sforza was just, is another question. At first glance this splendid figure seems completely classic — so closely was the spirit of the artist and the times approximating the antique — but further study reveals that the body has no detail except the coiffure, which might have been copied directly from a particular Greek or Roman statue, and that the features of the face, while conforming with classic standards, are quite original. Yet it is truly remarkable how closely Sansovino recaptured the underlying spirit of fourth-century Hellenic grace. Andrea del Sarto painted an adaption of this figure in the Chiostro dello Scalzo at Florence. He reversed the sword (here broken off for greater unity of outline) to point downward, placed the left foot on a step, increased the volume of the drapery, added fullness to the limbs, and reduced the size of the head in proportion to the body. All these changes are in keeping with the character of the fully developed art of the *cinquecento*, and remind us that Sansovino was for the most part distinctly an artist of the transition from the Early to the High Renaissance. The Prudence, too, is a fine figure with less idealized features, and an interesting disposition of the arms and legs. The seated Virtues of Hope (Fig. 40) and Faith, admirably characterized, recall the frequent representations of such seated Virtues of the *quattrocento*, and particularly those painted for the Mercanzia by Piero and Antonio Pollajuolo. The position of the legs and the drapery over them are similar even to the disposition of the folds over the thighs, but in keeping with the new spirit the torsos are left nude. The allegorical character of the Virtues is likewise more potently rendered by expression and gesture.

The attic is crowned with a group of two angels and God the Father in an arrangement surprisingly like that which Andrea had used for the Corbinelli altar. The angels differ only in being more static (because of their narrow pedestals), in the blown-out sleeve *motif*, and in bearing smaller candlesticks. In place of the semicircular relief of the Coronation, Sansovino has substituted an elaborately evolved shell and scroll base for the central figure. The intricacy and organic nature of this device may be reminiscences of Sansovino's experiments in the fantastic style of Portugal. All of these figures in the higher parts of the tomb are much less finished than the lower sculptures, and it may be inferred that the artist left the translation of them into marble to the hands of helpers.

The Madonna in a circular frame and the two cherubim heads which fill the lunette of the central niche are carefully designed and carried out, but are so obscured by the deep shadow of the vault above that one cannot see them well.

Of hardly less interest than the statues are the exquisitely carved and ever-varying arabesques (Fig. 41) which are lavishly used throughout the monument. The superlative feeling and remarkable technique of this ornament is unsurpassed. In comparison to the delicacy and free naturalism of this work, which vies with the finest of the Augustan period, the masterpieces of early renaissance ornament seem to have been chiseled in bronze. The four panels of the podium and the main frieze are decorated with heraldic devices of the Sforza.

Cardinal Girolamo Basso della Rovere, son of the sister of Sixtus IV, was as different from Ascanio Sforza as could be imagined. His relatives showered honors and benefices upon him, but he successfully evaded the wretched intrigues of the times and devoted his enormous wealth and his entire time to the benefit of his charges. When he died at Fabbrica a Castello in 1507, the tomb (Fig. 42) which Julius had ordered for the south wall of the choir, opposite the sepulchre of Ascanio, was probably well under construction.

In architectural form the two tombs are identical, and the angels and figures of God the Father were copied from the same models. The Virtues, however, differ, and Andrea made refinements in the figure of the cardinal and in the architectural ornament on the later monument. The seated Virtues are again Faith and Hope, characterized anew, and the standing Virtues are Fortitude (Fig. 43) and Temperance (Fig. 44). The latter represents one of the greatest achievements of Sansovino. The customary heavy woolen drapery is here supplanted by a diaphanous garment of soft, clinging stuff which reveals the beauty and grace of the figure beneath. Sansovino did not copy the antique but entered with amazing success into the spirit which generated the sculpture of Greece.

Similar success was achieved in the portrait of the cardinal (Fig. 42). While the nobly modeled face and expressive hands are certainly to be highly admired, it is the rhythmic outline of the figure and its expression of complete rest and peace that make it an outstanding effigy of its type. In ornament, Sansovino never excelled the panel of acanthus scrolls with two nude youths, which is so happily placed at eye-level under the main niche.

The dating of these monuments is comparatively simple: Ascanio died in May, 1505; Sansovino received a safe-conduct to go to Carrara to select marble on October 16, 1505.[12] On December 6 Sansovino contracted to have the marble transported from Avenza, the harbor of Carrara, to Rome, and on December 28 the artist received a safe-conduct order for the marble from Julius II.[13] Girolamo Basso died in 1507; and the tombs are mentioned as *in situ* by Albertini, who finished his guide of Rome on June 3, 1509.[14]

Tomb of Pietro de' Vincenti in Santa Maria d'Aracoeli

The wall sepulchre of Pietro de' Vincenti (Fig. 45), who died in 1504, is so closely related to the Sforza tomb, and has so frequently been attributed to Sansovino, that I must consider it at this point. All of the figures are copies of those on the Sforza tomb in Santa Maria del Popolo. A superficial comparison of photographs is sufficient to prove that they were not carved by the same hand. A comparison of the Virtues shows that the peculiar tubular heads are smaller, that the compressed mouths have long upper lips, that the attitudes are much more rigid, and that the drapery, instead of clinging to the limbs and revealing the form underneath, is chiseled out in angular gouges with somewhat the effect of flaked flint. An examination of the bishop's portrait and the relief of the Madonna reveals the same coarse and lifeless carving. The decorative carving is incomparably weaker in design and less delicate in execution.

By no means is this to be considered a preliminary study for the Sforza tomb; it is a monument, designed perhaps by Sansovino, but carried out entirely by an assistant working from the models made for the other tomb. I say that it may have been designed by the master because it appears unlikely that a sculptor who was independent of him would have been permitted to copy his creations while Sansovino was enjoying the patronage and protection of the pope. It would be of interest to know who the carver was. He may have been one of the assistants who followed Sansovino to Loreto.

The Pedimental Group of Santa Maria dell'Anima

In the pediment of the main façade of the church of the German nations in Rome, some forty feet above the street, is a seated *Madonna with the Christ Child* being adored by two nude men, or "souls" (Fig. 46). The Mary and Jesus are stylistically as early as Andrea's first years in Rome, indeed in many respects they are very close to the terra-cotta *Madonna* in the Bargello (Fig. 27). These figures have suffered considerably from exposure to the elements, but the "souls" are in such a sad state that one wonders at first if the round object beside the "soul" on the left may not be a cannon-ball. These "souls," so roughly finished, so sadly mutilated, take rank with the Bargello *Madonna* as the most expressive emotionally of Sansovino's creations. The group is an integral part of the architectural design, especially so because it represents the very name of Santa Maria dell'Anima, and since Giuliano da San Gallo designed the façade in 1506 [15] it is reasonable to suppose that he got his close friend, Sansovino, to make the statues at that time.

The Portrait of Cardinal Antonio del Monte

This medallion portrait in Berlin, which came from the Palazzo del Monte at Monte San Savino, is, according to Fabriczy,[16] a work by Andrea Sansovino of about the year 1511 or a little later. Vasari [17] gave it to Jacopo Sansovino, but internal evidence (its similarity of profile to the *Galba* and the curious nodule of drapery which represents the cardinal's hood) upholds Fabriczy's attribution. The mode of relief and delicate draughtsmanship remind one of the *Pietà* of the Corbinelli altar.

The Madonna and St. Anne in Sant'Agostino

Into this work (Fig. 47), done for a friend at the culmination of the artist's powers (he was fifty-two), Sansovino put all of his accumulated knowledge of expression and technique. Realism, classicism, roundness of form, softness of line, harmony of drapery, all qualities which Sansovino loved, join with his superlative ability to portray the deepest feelings between mother and child. The group is a masterpiece, and, in its province, the finest piece of sculpture of its century.[18]

The patron was the Luxemburger, Johann Goritz, apostolic protonotary, whom Müntz[19] called "Roman in heart and costume, and devotee of antiquity." Rome was flowing over with poets and writers: Molza, Blosio, Tebaldeo, Cavallo, Bembo, Baraballo, Mellini, Vida, Giovio, Longueil, Flaminio, Sadoleto, and a host of lesser fry. The literary men and their satellites often gathered in the villa of Goritz over the forum of Caesar. There in the midst of fragments of antique architecture and sculpture, learned discussions took place and grandiloquent poems were recited. Yet there must have been a great deal of merit in these reunions, since we find no less a scholar than Erasmus naming Goritz "the father of all the delights."[20] The treasures of this Maecenas were dispersed during the sack of Rome in 1527. The old man, broken-hearted, died shortly after in Mantua.

The base bears an inscription with the dedication, the title of Goritz, and the date 1512. Although the sculpture is now in a dark, cramped niche, it originally stood in the nave under the *Prophet Isaiah* of Raphael.[21] The group excited such enthusiasm amongst the numerous literary friends of Goritz that several of the verses they wrote about it were collected and published in 1524 under the title of *Coryciana.*[22]

The grouping is admirable: the Virgin is seated with the Child lying in her lap and looking up at His grandmother, who is smiling down at Him and fondling one of His feet with one hand while the other embraces the Virgin. The interplay of feeling is quite equal to the masterful interweaving of the three figures.

As in his earlier representations of the Madonna, Sansovino has heightened the internal unity by maintaining a close family resemblance in the three figures. Of interest, too, are the easy and graceful postures, which the sculptor has achieved by setting Anne somewhat higher (with a book under her feet, which, no doubt, is a tribute to the literary status of Goritz). The statement by Bode [23] that the composition is too obviously inspired by Leonardo is so absurd that it needs no formal refutation. Let the reader compare!

This group is at once Sansovino's most classic and most perfect work. No other sculpture of the Renaissance better realizes the golden mean of naturalism and idealism. The head of Mary (Fig. 48) is a poem of rhythmic lines and harmonious masses. It is purely classic. Yet what kind of classic? Where in the whole wide realm of Greek or Roman art can one find a model for this head? It cannot be done. One is forced to conclude that Sansovino, with the aid of a few second-rate antiques, was able to recreate, by sheer genius, works that belong in spirit to the age of Praxiteles!

SANSOVINO AT LORETO, AND HIS LATEST SCULPTURE

LORETO is a town about fifteen miles south of Ancona. It is on the crest of a high hill and is a mile and a half from the shore of the Adriatic. The town owes its importance solely to the presence of the Holy House of the Virgin. During the course of the fourteenth and fifteenth centuries a legend grew up that a tiny chapel which occupied the hilltop was in reality the house in which the Mother of Our Lord was born and brought up. There she received the annunciation. There, too, she had lived after the ascension of her Son. It is a small rectangular structure of brick and stone, measuring twenty-eight by twelve and a half feet in height. The legend relates that this was the Virgin's house in Nazareth, over which the Empress Helena built a basilica in 336. After the fall of the kingdom of Jerusalem, the Turks threatened to destroy the sacred structure. But God sent angels on the night of May 9, 1291, and they carried the house through the air, and set it down the next morning on a hill near Tersatto in Dalmatia. There it rested three years and caused many miracles. On December 10, 1294, angels again flew with the house and, traversing the Adriatic, placed it in a grove of laurel trees (hence the name Loreto) near Recanati. Now the two brothers who owned the grove began to quarrel over the valuable offerings left by pilgrims. And since the locality was disreputable, angels came a third time, and moved the building to the top of a high hill in the midst of the public road where no man might claim ownership. And there it is today, although some unbelievers claim to have documentary proof that a church had occupied the

identical site for a hundred years before 1295, the date of the
final move. Loreto became the most popular of the places of
pilgrimage devoted to the cult of Mary in late medieval and
renaissance times. For obvious reasons the present pope has declared the Madonna of Loreto the patron of aviation, and a large
landing field has been constructed in the valley below the town.

Pope Paul II (in 1468) began to build a late Gothic church
over the Santa Casa in gratitude for having here been cured of
the plague when he was still a cardinal. Previously the shrine
had been sheltered by a simple, rectangular structure. As its
architects before the coming of Bramante in 1509 the church at
Loreto boasted Giuliano da Majano, Baccio Pontelli, Giuliano da
San Gallo, and Francesco di Giorgio Martini. The sacristies
were frescoed by Melozzo da Forlì (and assistants) and Luca
Signorelli. Girolamo Basso della Rovere, whose tomb Sansovino
made in Sta. Maria del Popolo, had been the administrator of
Loreto from 1476 to 1507.

Sansovino may have been engaged in profitable work during
the year 1512, for he did not accept an offer of June 23, 1512, by
the Operai di Santa Maria del Fiore to do two statues of the
Apostles Matthew and Thaddeus.[1] Probably he refused the
offer of the cathedral authorities because he hoped to succeed
Giancristoforo Romano, who died on May 31, 1512, as master of
the works at Loreto. His hopes were well founded, for Antonio
Ciocchi del Monte San Savino, his fellow townsman, had been
governor of the sanctuary since 1507, and became its first cardinal
protector when he received the hat in 1512. In any case, on
June 22, 1513, Leo X issued a brief making Andrea "capo e
Maestro generale della fabbrica Loretana e dell' opera di scultura
per l'ornamento della Santa Casa."[2]

As master of the works, Sansovino found three principal
duties awaiting him: to build a palace to house the functionaries

connected with the shrine, to finish the pilgrimage church —
which was in a sorry state — and to case the Santa Casa in an
elaborate sheathing of carved marble. The brief in which Leo X
appointed Andrea to the position gave him supreme authority in
everything connected with these works. He was in charge of all
the masters and workmen and could hire and dismiss them as he
wished. He was to supervise the obtaining of marble and other
necessary materials. Furthermore, he was to make plans for the
buildings, supervise the construction, and demolish or change all
that he deemed ill-made. This last provision is important, for it
proves that Sansovino was in nowise bound to follow designs
left by Bramante.[3] His salary was set at the rate of 15 ducats
a month when he was at Loreto, and 6 per month when he was
absent, if he was not absent more than four months a year. Any
longer vacation was without pay. In addition, he was to receive
extra payment for the sculpture that he did for the Santa Casa, a
house, and provisions for his servant and horse.

During the year 1514 the documents of the Santa Casa begin
to speak of Sansovino, and note that he was paid for five days at
Cararra and twenty at Rome in addition to his salary at Loreto.[4]
On May 3, 1514, the first shipload of marble arrived in Ancona
from Carrara.[5] Then his salary was paid regularly, without any
diminution for absence, up to July 2, 1516, which indicates that
for two years he was busy amassing supplies of building material
for the enormous projects. Leo X was most anxious to speed up
construction. On June 14, 1513, out of the 4,791 ducats in the
alms box he designated 2,000 for building. We also find briefs
giving permission to cut down communal and private woods,
settling disputes between the commune of Recanati and the Santa
Casa over the timber supply, and begging the Emperor Maxi-
milian to donate wood in the neighborhood of Fiume. Great
quantities of fuel were needed for stoking the lime furnaces and

brick kilns. Finally, on January 17, 1517, the pope sent a brief
stating that Sansovino might remove shrubs and saplings wherever he wished, and that all landowners were to give him ready
access to their lands and were not to interfere with the cutting
or transportation of the wood.[6]

During this time Sansovino built piers to fortify the arches
of the crossing so that the dome of the basilica might be erected
safely. He carried on the building of the palace at a goodly pace,
as the payments for walls, vaults, and staircases testify.

After July 1, 1515, when Leo X designated Cardinal Bibiena
Procuratore Generale of the Santa Casa with absolute power,
Sansovino began little by little to lose his authority. Already
on December 8, 1514, Bibiena had become cardinal protector of
Loreto. After the second appointment Bibiena's will was law.
The problems arising out of this change in administration culminated in an official investigation. Pope Leo X, in a brief of
January 18, 1517, charged Antonio da San Gallo the Younger
to inspect all of the work which was under way at Loreto. He
ordered Sansovino to assist San Gallo in every way during this
inspection.[7] San Gallo arrived early in April at Loreto and made
his inspection, then Sansovino went to Rome for several days "to
consult Monsignor Raffaele [Bibiena], our protector, about the
affairs of the building."[8]

The pope was dissatisfied with the progress at Loreto. In
order that Sansovino might begin work on the sculptural decoration of the shrine, he removed him from the charge of master of
architecture, and confined his duties to the mastery of the carving ("maestria di scalpello"). Pressure was exerted to hasten all
work at Loreto. To that end another architect, Cristoforo di
Simone Resse (or Resecco) of Imola, was dispatched from Rome.
Resse arrived at Loreto February 21, 1518, and carried on the
construction work until his death on June 14, 1522. As architect,

his work was not superior to his predecessor's; as a director of construction, he was such an inferior manager that he left his family in debt 2,138 florins to the Santa Casa.

The account books of the Santa Casa show that except for three and a half months in 1517 (June 17 to October 1) and three months in 1518 (July to September) Sansovino remained at Loreto during this period up to July 10, 1519, when comes a lapse in the payment of his monthly stipend of 15 ducats. On the following January 30 (1520), he is credited with 20 ducats "for the two and a half months from the 13th of November to this day. And from now on, in accordance with the orders from Rome of Monsignor Reverendo [Cardinal Bibiena] and Messer Cynthio, we are not to pay any more expenses for him and his servant." [9] Doubtless the authorities felt that Sansovino's salary was too high since they had to maintain another man as *capo maestro*. The sculptor, however, saw the matter in a different light and appealed to the pope. Leo X ordered a lump sum of over 225 ducats paid Andrea on January 1, 1512.[10] On the December 20 preceding, the pope had written a letter [11] confirming Sansovino's appointment and praising him highly. The monthly stipend was, however, reduced to 10 ducats. In a letter [12] from Giuliano Ridolfi, called the Priore di Capua, who had succeeded Cardinal Bibiena as protector on that prelate's demise (November, 1520), the terms of the new agreement were repeated. In addition to the 10 ducats a month Andrea was to retain his house, but was not to receive provisions for himself or servant.[13] The decision of the pope was a compromise: Sansovino was retained, but was to receive a reduced salary commensurate to his reduced duties.

Since the documents mentioned above also refer to Sansovino's reliefs for the Santa Casa and the payments therefor, it now behooves us to consider when, and the conditions under which, they were done. From the two letters and the account books [14] the following facts are clear: first, he was to be paid 500 ducats for each story (complete panel), which was to be done well and by his own hand; second, each story (*storia*) was to be composed of two squares (*quadri*); third, he was to receive a third of the pay upon beginning each story, a third when half finished, and the final third when the work was done; fourth, the stories of the *Annunciation* and the *Birth of Christ* [15] were to be done within three years. The two reliefs (the *Annunciation* and the *Birth of Christ*) were completed by May 30, 1524, according to the credit book,[16] which also states that one *quadro* (that is one half) of each relief had been turned over to the authorities of the Santa Casa earlier than this. One half (each relief is made up of two slightly different sized slabs of marble) of each story was probably made during the years 1517–1520 and paid for at the end of 1520 or in January, 1521.[17] Then Sansovino was paid 166⅔ ducats on June 24, 1521,[18] for beginning a new story, that is to say one of the remaining *quadri*. On June 19, 1522,[19] he received a like sum for the *quadro* finished, the completion of which would be the equivalent of the half-way payment of a third. Both stories had been completed and turned over to the administration of the Santa Casa when full payment was made on June 30, 1524.[20] The text of Document XVI leaves no room for doubt that Sansovino executed a half of each relief before completing either. This would explain the insistence of the Priore di Capua [21] "that he thus continue each story, beginning one, then when it was finished, the other." Clearly the Priore was irritated by the sculptor's mode of procedure. Sansovino took more than the stipulated three years to finish the reliefs, but this was not his fault, because the advent of a new pope, the austere Hadrian VI, soon put a stop to all work on the Santa Casa. Hadrian was elected January 9, 1522; Sansovino left Loreto at the end of the following June and did not return until

March 28, 1523.[22] He again quitted Loreto on July 1, 1523, because there was no work in progress.[23] This probably means that there was no money to pay Andrea's salary, for Hadrian had "borrowed" the considerable sum of 4,100 ducats from the account of the Santa Casa.[24] The Dutch pope was no friend of artists. Shortly after, another Medici became the successor of St. Peter (November 19, 1523), and things took a sudden turn for the better. Indeed Clement VII not only reinstated Sansovino on December 24, 1523, but even restored him to his earlier rank as master of the works, that is as architect as well as sculptor.[25] In 1524 [26] he was working on a third relief, the *Marriage of the Virgin*, and indeed on June 24, 1527, he received 166⅔ ducats as a third payment. The same entry [27] states that he was making the story of two *quadri*, and that one of them was almost finished. During these years Andrea spent little time at Loreto "for fear of the plague," [28] but the real reason was that he was getting old and wanted to stay in Tuscany. This desire is manifest in his letters to Michelangelo.[29] June 29, 1527, the account book notes that "he parted [from Loreto] according to his wont," [30] and this is the last notice of his presence at Loreto.

On October 11, 1532, Antonio da San Gallo adjudged that the heirs of Master Andrea should receive 392 ducats for "one part of the story of the *Marriage of the Madonna*, which that master had left unfinished upon his death." [31]

In the earliest of the account books of Loreto that have to do with the decoration of the casing of the Santa Casa (Book "B," 1517–1518), Baccio Bandinelli received pay as an assistant to Andrea.[32] He drew money in advance for the relief of the *Birth of the Virgin* in 1519, fled from Ancona, where he was working, and left the relief quite unfinished.[33] In 1524–1525 he was back at Ancona and drew pay for work on the Santa Casa, but it appears that in 1526–1527 Baccio had left again even further in debt (795 ducats). Raffaele da Montelupo completed the relief in 1533 [34] and was paid 600 ducats, so that we may judge that Baccio had done somewhat more than a half of the whole scene, since 750 ducats was the price for a complete *quadro* at that time. The account book [35] says that two *quadri* were returned to Loreto from Ancona, which indicates that he had finished one half and begun the second.

Domenico dell'Amia da Bologna, sculptor, received 210 ducats in 1517 or 1518,[36] and there are further entries of payments to him during 1519 and 1520. He is then mentioned in the documents as being away at Rome and elsewhere, when he was finishing his large statue of Leo X, now in the church of the Aracoeli, Rome, but in 1525 he was credited with two *quadri* of the *Death of the Virgin*.[37] Domenico also moved his house and work to Ancona when Bandinelli went there.[38]

In 1519 Simone Cioli da Settignano received a salary of 7 ducats and 20 soldi per month for service as *scarpellino*. Again in 1533, 1534, and 1535 he drew pay for the ornamentation of the Santa Casa and for *un puttino*.[39]

From two entries dating from October, 1533,[40] it appears that Raffaele da Montelupo received 1,500 ducats for the *Epiphany*, "fatto da tutto punto da lui," 600 for finishing the *Birth of the Virgin*, and 400 for the small panel of the *Visitation*. The same documents say that Tribolo got 250 ducats for finishing the half of the *Marriage of the Virgin* left unfinished by Sansovino, 750 for the other half of the same scene, 350 for five *putti*, and 750 for one half of the *Translation of the Santa Casa*. Likewise, Francesco di Giuliano da San Gallo (the documents always read "di Vicenzo") received 400 ducats for the small panel of the *Presentation*, and 740 for one half of the *Translation of the Santa Casa*. Furthermore, Dossi [41] says that 400 ducats were paid Domenico dell'Amia, Tribolo, and San Gallo for finishing the

Death of the Virgin on December 31, 1536; and that 140 ducats were given Tribolo, Raffaele, and San Gallo for two more *putti*. Dossi believed that San Gallo did the two *putti* but that the pay was made to all three in order to equalize their work on other sculptures.

The monumental casing of the Santa Casa (Fig. 49) was not erected until 1533 or 1534; and it was not until June 18, 1537, that the balustrade was added.[42] The statues of the Prophets and Sibyls were still lacking.

I had not intended to write a history of the adornment of the Santa Casa, but such a partial summary is a necessary prelude to a consideration of Sansovino's part in the designing of those scenes which he did not execute.

Andrea Sansovino invented and executed the *Annunciation* (Fig. 50) and the *Adoration of the Shepherds* (Fig. 51); he executed about a half of the *Marriage* (Fig. 52), which was finished by Tribolo, probably according to the original design, which must have been available. Dell'Amia may have designed the scene of the *Death of the Virgin*. On the other hand, there is evidence that Baccio made his own design for the *Birth of Mary* in a series of study sketches by him in the Uffizi.[43] No one of the drawings represents the scene as executed, but the general composition is similar in all three, and many of the figures, which were carved, are shown in the drawings, including the maid kneeling in front of the basin in the half that was executed by Raffaele. In the same way, it would seem probable that Tribolo followed — not too closely, however — Sansovino's design for the *Marriage* when completing it. All of these later sculptors who worked at Loreto after Sansovino's death in 1529 were mature artists of some reputation, and it is unlikely that they adhered closely to any models which Sansovino may have left, yet the general uniformity of the mode of relief, the persistence of the same types throughout the series, and the presence of certain peculiarities of Sansovino (especially the curious cloud convention) make it probable that they were influenced strongly by Sansovino's designs.

The statues of the Prophets and Sybils were made by Girolamo and Aurelio Lombardi, and Giovanni Battista and Tommaso della Porta.[44]

The Annunciation

One must be sympathetic to the spirit of ingenuity which permeates the creations of the sixteenth century to appreciate fully the content and beauty of this picture — for such it is, a relief picture in marble (Figs. 49 and 50). Let Giorgio Vasari be our guide.[45]

> The *Annunciation* is of indescribable grace, the Virgin being intent upon the salutation, and the angel kneeling seems not of marble but truly celestial, as the *Ave Maria* issues from his lips. Two other angels in relief are in the company of Gabriel, one accompanying him and the other flying. Two more advance from behind a building, and seem alive; and resting on a marble cloud . . . are cherubs, sustaining God the Father, who is sending the Holy Spirit by a marble ray, which looks most natural. So also is the dove representing the Holy Spirit. A vase full of flowers in this work is of indescribable beauty and delicate carving, and indeed Andrea's achievement cannot be praised sufficiently in the angel's plumage, hair, graceful features and draperies, and, in fact, in everything.

Even more illuminating is Vasari's answer in a letter to Martino Basso, who had sent him a drawing to criticize.[46]

> I believe that it would be most difficult to find such a fine setting (*casamento*) as M. Andrea Sansovino made at Loreto on the front side of the Chapel of the Madonna, in that *Annunciation* of his, wherein a row of columns on pedestals, bearing arches, creates a beautiful flight of openings (*isfuggimento di trafori*), rich and varied. Besides, those clouds full of boys make a miraculous sight with the Holy Spirit.

In comparison with Andrea's design, Vasari condemns the drawing of Basso as follows: "It seems to me that those two

figures, so bare and alone, are like two poor little eels in a
great big kettle." Simplicity, we see, was not a virtue in the
cinquecento. Andrea's great success lay in his ability to include
all the variety and richness which the taste of his contemporaries
demanded, and at the same time tell the story in such a direct
and forcible way that the incidental detail does not disturb the
spectator. Indeed, after he has taken in the drama of the scene,
the spectator may experience genuine delight in observing the
fine flight of columns, the magnificent lilies, the cat full of
curiosity, the tree with its clinging vine, the cupboard full of
books and vases, and the graceful winged boys in their varied
activities. The design is admirable; one can question only the
propriety of reproducing it in marble. But then, nearly all reliefs
are pictorial by nature. One might just as well question the
Florentine custom of making pictures which look like paintings of
reliefs or even like sculpture in the round!

The sequence of three angels which culminates in the figure
of Gabriel is one of the most effective examples of the continuous
method of narration. The possibility of offending the laws of
nature was adroitly avoided by giving the archangel two angel
attendants who occupy positions and attitudes which but a
moment before were those of Gabriel. So is produced a magnificent sense of the swift gliding motion of the messenger of God.

The Adoration of the Shepherds

Quite as dramatic, and more plastic in effect — indeed the
figures seem to be actors on a narrow stage with architectural
properties and a back drop — is Sansovino's relief of the *Presepio*
(Fig. 51). The elements are traditional; the composition is
completely new. One searches in vain for a similar presentation
of the subject in the *quattrocento*. All interest centers upon the
Christ Child, a veritable baby God, so strong, so sure, so com-

manding! Angels fly above, gaily singing hosannas; one goes to tell an expectant shepherd the glad news. Three shepherds come hurrying in from the left, and Joseph from the right. The ox and ass show great interest. It is a *Presepio* of finest spirit.

Marcel Reymond [47] wrote a finely phrased appreciation of this relief: "Les jolies recherches de mouvements de Sansovino ne devraient pas non plus provoquer le blâme, mais être admirées comme une très intéressante nouveauté artistique, qui n'a pas ici du reste le défaut d'être en désaccord avec le motif de l'Adoration des bergers, motif qui n'est vraiment bien exprimé que par des figures en mouvement."

The Marriage of the Virgin

Without any doubt the carving on this piece (Fig. 52), for which Andrea was paid 392 ducats, is restricted to the *quadro* to the left. The figures of that half must have been almost finished, yet all, except the high priest, show signs of finishing by another hand. The women to the left are beautifully varied in pose, but Tribolo made them of heavier proportions than Andrea intended, and thereby lost much of the grace of the group.

The Madonna of Santa Maria in Porta Paradisi

In 1518 Leo X had the Piazza del Popolo enlarged, but even after these works it was far from having the grand area of today. At the same time he began the piercing of a street (the Via di Ripetta) from the Piazza del Popolo through vineyards and fields toward the Mausoleum of Augustus.

En lan 1518 par commandement du pape Léon X, fut commence la strada de notre dame de populo depuys liglise S. Yves joucques audit populo et fut achevée en lan 1519 et fut taille la maison du cardinal Ursin qui est pres du dict populo pour passez par elle et par les vignes et estoint maistres de lestrade de Rome Misser Bartolomeo de lavale et Misser Ramondo Capo de ferro et nota que ont fait poyer largent au cortisanes de Rome pour fere ladite strade.[48]

The Via del Babuino was probably put through at this time too, for an inscription of 1525 alludes to the Via Flaminia, *trifariam divisam* at its entry into the city. Leo X confided the execution of this plan to Raphael Santi and Antonio da San Gallo the Younger, who were then the *maestri di strada*.

Now the small church of Santa Maria in Porta Paradisi has carved over its portal on the Via di Ripetta the following inscription: "ECCLA S. M. PORTAE PARADISI ET LIBERATRICIS PESTILENTIAE ANNO DOMINI MDXXIII"; and since the Via di Ripetta was not constructed until after 1518, it is reasonable to conclude that 1523 is the true date of the erection of this church. Is it possible that Andrea Sansovino was in Rome at this time? The account books at Loreto testify that he left there at the end of June, 1522, and returned at the end of March, 1523, to stay until July 1, 1523, after which he was absent until December, 1523.[49] In other words, Sansovino was occupied at Loreto only three months during the year and a half following June, 1522. We have direct evidence that he was in Rome at the end of this period.[50] The only other work that we know to have occupied him during this time was the design of the singing gallery and pulpit of Sant' Agostino in Monte San Savino, and the cloister adjoining that church. This cannot have occupied him long, for the work was not carried out until ten years later.[51] Chronologically, then, there is no objection to attributing the *Madonna and Child* group (Fig. 53) to Andrea.

It is conceived in the same broad and noble spirit as the group in Sant'Agostino at Rome, but it shows an even closer resemblance to the figures in Andrea's design for the tomb of Leo X (Fig. 73), the making of which, by the way, is yet another bit of circumstantial evidence that Sansovino lived in Rome during this period. The anatomy of the Child and the rich disposition of the limbs are especially reminiscent of the St. Anne group (Fig.

47) in Sant'Agostino. The treatment of the drapery is new, as is the posture. Compare the figures on the tomb drawing referred to above (Fig. 73). The Hope (at the upper right) is in a strikingly similar posture to this *Madonna*. Notice the likeness of the folds which fall from the left hip of Faith (in the lower left) to those falling from the Virgin's left shoulder. Compare also the equally complicated posture of the Virgin in the *Annunciation* (Fig. 50), and the head-dresses, which are of the same type. There are many similarities in drapery treatment in the drawing, the Loreto reliefs, and the work now under consideration.

The marble is highly polished and has a dark patina like the group done for Goritz.

The St. Roch at Battifolle

"For a German priest, a friend, he did a St. Roch of life-size, in terra-cotta, and very beautiful. This priest had it placed in the church of Battifolle in the territory of Arezzo. It was Andrea's last sculpture."[52] I believe that Vasari is right concerning the date of this painted terra-cotta *St. Roch* (Figs. 54 and 55), which is still to be found in the church of S. Quirico at Battifolle between Arezzo and Monte San Savino, but the Aretine errs regarding its size, for it measures but little more than a meter in height.[53] The easy attitude with one foot raised, the natural disposition of the arms, and the facial type, which is the same as that used for Joseph in the *Adoration* (Fig. 51), place this work very late in the artist's career.

THE ARCHITECTURE OF ANDREA SANSOVINO

ALTHOUGH Andrea Sansovino was not one of the universal geniuses of the Renaissance, he did win fame in two great creative fields, sculpture and architecture. To the latter art he devoted much time and effort, especially during the late years of his life. Doubtless his greatest success as an architect was in the field of sculptural architecture, the designing of tombs and altars. But he planned many buildings, and although few are the plans that were carried out and fewer the buildings that have come down to us, there remains a sufficient body of architecture from which to judge his style.

Vasari lists the building activities of Andrea in Florence, Arezzo, Monte San Savino, Loreto, and Portugal. Documentary evidence adds work at Jesi. From those monuments which are preserved and from his sculpture and drawings one can form a good idea of Andrea's ability as an architect. Let us consider the works themselves and some of the problems connected with them.

The first difficulty is well introduced by the following quotation from Vasari:[1]

Turning to sculpture, Sansovino did two capitals of pilasters in his youth for Cronaca, for the sacristy of Sto. Spirito, which brought him great fame, and led to his being employed to make the anteroom between the sacristy and the church [Fig. 57]. The place being narrow, Andrea had to display his resources. He constructed two rows of six round columns in *macigno* of the Corinthian order, laying the architraves, friezes, and cornices upon them, and making a barrel vault of the same stone with richly and variously carved compartments, a much admired novelty. It is true that the work would be better if the compartments forming the divisions of the squares and circles had been in a line with the columns, a thing which it would have been easy to do. Some of his old friends, however, have informed me that he defended this, saying that he had copied the Rotonda (the Pantheon) at Rome, where the ribs from the circular opening in the center form the compartments, and then gradually diminish, and that the ribs there are not in line with the columns. He added that if the builder of the Rotonda, which is the best designed and proportioned temple there is, did not take these things into account in a vault of greater size and importance, it was of even less importance on a smaller scale.

In December, 1489, Giuliano da San Gallo received 77 florins and 8 soldi for making a model of the sacristy of Sto. Spirito.[2] In December, 1490, the Opera di Sto. Spirito paid to Andrea di Nicolò, sculptor, 45 florins and 10 soldi.[3] Between February 27, 1490, and October 10, 1492, the shops of Giovanni di Betto and Simone del Caprina delivered forty capitals to the Opera for the sacristy and the Cappella Barbadori, of which Simone sent only three. The inference that all of these capitals were for the sacristy and the Cappella Barbadori is Signor Botto's. Some of them may have been for the antesacristy or other work connected with the church. The documents are silent on this point; they merely record the deliveries and payments. On the ninth day of March, 1493, the members of the Opera met with Simone del Pollajuolo, Giuliano da San Gallo, Giovanni di Betto, Salvi d'Andrea, and Pagno d'Antonio to decide whether to build the vault, "which must be made before one enters the sacristy where the twelve columns have been put" of cement or brick or carved stone (Fig. 57). All agreed that since the work had been begun so richly and with so many columns the vault should be made of stone and coffered with roses or some other suitable design. Simone and Giuliano showed Pietro de' Medici some designs for it.[4]

The question is: how much of the statement of Vasari is credible? In the first edition of the *Lives* (1550) the Aretine does not mention the sacristy vestibule in any way, but speaks of the two capitals in the sacristy itself. Some time during the next eighteen years (1550-1568) "some old friend" of Sansovino told

Vasari the story which he quotes. The old friend may have been Jacopo Tatti or Baccio Bandinelli; in any case, Vasari's story is precise and clear in meaning. Any modifications of it must be well founded.

To begin with, Stechow-Göttingen has convincingly identified the two sacristy capitals (Fig. 56), which he points out are cold and academic, timid beginner's work in comparison with the other capitals by Giuliano da San Gallo.[5] To continue, the document of March 9, 1493, definitely proves that Sansovino was responsible neither for the execution nor the working design of the coffered barrel vault of the vestibule (Fig. 57). This is reasonable since the figures and ornamental carving do not resemble any well accepted work of his. We have left two parts of the antesacristy for attribution to Andrea, namely the general design and the columns. For several reasons I believe that Sansovino was the creator of the main design and the colonnade. First, as I have said above, Vasari's words ring true, and no opinion based upon style alone has validity in this case, for the style of the old and virile Giuliano might well dominate the creations of either Sansovino or Cronaca. Yet even the style argues *for* Sansovino rather than *against* him: the novelty of free-standing (not engaged) colonnades supporting what is, in effect, a free-standing vault is quite in keeping with the eccentric architecture which the sculptor designed in later years. The use of the wider central intercolumniation was often a part of Andrea's design — in the Corbinelli altar, in the Sta. Maria del Popolo tombs, and at Jesi. The four doorways may all be attributed to Giuliano, since he did the sacristy and presumably, therefore, the most important portal, of which the other three are copies. Now to consider the style of the columns: there is nothing unusual in the bases, in the proportions of the shafts, or, indeed, in the capitals, about which so much has been written. They are all of one general type, that which is frequently termed the Mars Ultor capital, and of which there were good examples in the baptistry of S. Giovanni and in S. Miniato. Two of these capitals, however — those in the northeast corner — differ from the others in detail and in having carved designs on their abacus mouldings. Moreover, they lack the coherence and tectonic expression of the others. Somehow a story grew up (after the design of the vestibule had been attributed to Cronaca, or Giuliano da San Gallo, or both) that Sansovino did these two capitals. Perhaps the inventor of the idea misread Vasari; in any case, the attribution is unsatisfactory.

Forty-five florins and 10 soldi would have been a lot of money to pay Andrea di Nicolò for the model of the two sacristy capitals — or even for the carving of them — if Signor Botto would have Cronaca paid only 13 florins for designing the sacristy vestibule! The records of Sto. Spirito are not complete, and it is possible that Sansovino might have been paid more, but I believe that the above considerable sum has to do with his work in the antesacristy.

Finally the conference of March 9, 1493 was convened to ask the opinion of "several clever masters, amongst whom were Simone del Pollajuolo, Giuliano da San Gallo, Giovanni di Betto, Salvi d'Andrea, and Pagno d'Antonio," as to how to complete the vestibule where the twelve columns were standing. The very formality of the meeting appears to imply that this was the renewal of a project which had been dropped for some time, and the lack of distinction amongst the "several clever masters" — no one is singled out as the author of the work — suggests that the original architect was absent. Sansovino was probably in Portugal at that time.

In summary, I believe Vasari's account may be substantiated in the following way: Sansovino designed the two sacristy capitals referred to above, and drew up general plans for the antesacristy.

These plans must have indicated the main lines of the vault coffering. After the columns were up, it would appear that work was arrested, and that Sansovino left Florence before it was resumed, as related in the above-mentioned document.

If Sansovino was the architect of this vestibule, as I believe he was, it is necessary to assume that he was a disciple of Giuliano da San Gallo. The conception of the finely proportioned little corridor is decidedly in San Gallo's vein. To prove this, one has only to compare it with the open loggia on the front of the Villa of Poggio a Cajano by Giuliano. Indeed, the accumulative indications that Sansovino was a pupil of San Gallo in architecture are convincing. Dr. Middeldorf[6] believes that Sansovino modeled the interesting terra-cotta relief on the entablature of the Poggio a Cajano arcade. If he did, Andrea was probably connected with San Gallo at least as early as 1485. Also there is the probability that Sansovino owed the commission of his Roman tombs to the architect, who was a close friend of Pope Julius. A further possible connection between the two artists is to be found in the pedimental group of Santa Maria dell'Anima. And finally, it must be recognized that throughout his career Sansovino continued to design architecture in a *quattrocento* style similar to Giuliano's.

Likewise a close connection between Andrea and Simone del Pollajuolo (il Cronaca) may be assumed from the similarity of their styles. Furthermore, in Berlin [7] there is a drawing of Simone which depicts four sprigs of floral ornament, two cornices — each of which is labeled "questa chornice da simone" — and an altar base with the inscription, "Lo basimento dello altare dasimone d[ella] mano d[i] maestro andrea." The altar is of fine proportions and has well disposed mouldings of delicate outline. The base mouldings are made richer than any of Andrea's by the addition of a *cyma reversa*; nevertheless it seems reasonable to identify the "maestro andrea" with Sansovino. Simone was but three years older than Andrea, both had training in the shop of Antonio Pollajuolo according to Vasari, both were working for the churches of Santo Spirito and Santa Maria del Fiore at the same time, and both had numerous contacts with Giuliano da San Gallo.

On January 5, 1491, Sansovino was listed as a member of the commission to judge projects for finishing the façade of Santa Maria del Fiore.[8]

Of Andrea's buildings in Portugal I have already written in a previous chapter. Suffice it to repeat here that there is no architecture in that land which may reasonably be attributed to him.

Fabriczy[9] attributed to Andrea Sansovino two palaces in Rome: the Casino di Papa Giulio on the Via Flaminia, and the Palazzo Lante (Medici), which Leo X built for his brother, Giuliano de' Medici. These works Fabriczy assigned to the years 1511–1520. As a matter of fact, we do hear nothing of Andrea for the three years preceding 1512. During that period he signed no works, nor does he appear in any documents. The last preceding notice concerning Andrea is in June, 1509, when Albertini mentioned the tombs in the choir of Sta. Maria del Popolo as *in situ*. Therefore the presumption that Sansovino was in Rome engaged on important building projects is not unreasonable, since he had acquired a reputation as an architect by 1513, when Leo X appointed him master of the works at Loreto. Let us consider the monuments Fabriczy credited to Andrea.

Vasari[10] said in the life of Jacopo Sansovino: "For Cardinal Antonio di Monte he [Jacopo] began a large structure at his [Cardinal Antonio's] villa on the Acqua Vergine outside Rome." Fabriczy identified this structure with the Casino di Papa Giulio after Raffaele Erculei[11] had written an article in which he had come to the same conclusion. Now Fabriczy recognized that the building was not in the style of Jacopo Sansovino, therefore he thought that Vasari had confused the name of the designer, who, when the correction should have been made, would be found to be Andrea Sansovino. Curiously enough, there is a stylistic similarity to Andrea's architecture, but any hope of proving the charming and eccentric little palace to be by Andrea has vanished into thin air, since documents have come to light [12] which conclusively prove that the palace dates from the second half of the sixteenth century. Most of the lower story was probably built by Bartolomeo Ammannati in connection with the fountain which he designed on the corner for Julius III, and the upper story was not constructed until 1561–1564. The structure built by Jacopo Sansovino may have been a loggia "with marble columns" which stood on the site of the present palace, or it may have been a house which formerly stood on the other side of the Via Flaminia, or it may have been some other structure on the extensive *vigna*. In any case, it would be fantastic to attribute to Andrea a work which Vasari said Jacopo did when we do not know that work.

As for the Lante palace, Fabriczy, and compilers of guide books who have followed him, have never adduced stylistic or documentary evidence to support the attribution. It is not at all surprising that this evidence has not been forthcoming, since the palace is not in Andrea's style.

Müntz [13] declared that Andrea Sansovino was one of the collaborators of Raphael when he took charge of the construction of St. Peters after the death of Bramante in 1514. This indicates that Sansovino had achieved a reputation as an architect. Indeed, his appointment as master of architecture and sculpture at Loreto in 1513 proves that.[14]

One of the first tasks of Andrea at Loreto was to strengthen the supports for the great dome which Bramante had planned to build directly above the Santa Casa at the crossing of the church. Although as yet they supported no dome, their construction had been so bad that they were threatening to collapse of their own weight. Sansovino evolved many plans for remedying this defect, as some drawings in the Uffizi testify. In 1514 he erected a supporting wall on the east side,[15] but did not continue with the construction of the dome because the structure still showed signs of instability.

During his first three years at Loreto, Sansovino carried on the building of the palace of the canons at a fair pace. Walls, vaults, windows, doors, stairs, and three piers were constructed under his direction.[16] Indeed, he must have built quite a bit of the body of the existing palace. Vasari [17] says that he carried out the designs of Bramante. When Antonio da San Gallo made his tour of inspection in April, 1517,[18] he condemned this work and stated that it would have to be corrected. It is doubtful whether any of the present arcade in front of the palace was done by Andrea, although it is barely possible that the three piers mentioned in the documents are those nearest the church.

Judging from the numerous payments to *scarpellini*, a goodly portion of the casing of the Santa Casa (Fig. 49) was executed under Sansovino. It was not erected until 1533–1534. Again Vasari [19] states that he merely carried out the plans of Bramante. Stylistic evidence corroborates the Aretine's statement. Furthermore, Vasari probably obtained this information from a trustworthy source, Girolamo Campagna, who had worked under Andrea at Loreto when a youth.

In July, 1519, Sansovino designed the courtyard of the Palazzo del Comune at Jesi, which is about twenty miles distant from Loreto. Giovanni di Gabriele da Como was in charge of the actual construction.[20]

The sober yet elegant Palazzo del Comune was built by Francesco di Giorgio Martini during the years 1486 to 1498. But he had not been able to complete the building, to which Sansovino finally gave an arcaded courtyard.

The condition of the edifice was bad when I made some snapshots in 1932. Now, however, it is being restored in order to become the civic museum. As such, it will be a fitting home for the fine paintings of Lorenzo Lotto which Jesi boasts.

There are three stories facing the courtyard (Fig. 58). The ground story has a severe order of piers (Fig. 59) supporting an arcade which is groin-vaulted. The principal floor employs a graceful variation of the Corinthian order (Fig. 60), while the top story has simple arched openings to correspond to the arcades below. At all three levels the long sides are composed of four similar round arches, and the short sides of two such round arches flanking a wider, central arch. The corner piers of the principal floor are most ingeniously formed of a square pier with half-columns sunk into it to respond to the arches of the colonnade. The materials used are brick — plastered over — and yellow Verona marble.

Two years later Sansovino was recalled to Jesi to design towers for the city walls.[21]

A simple house (Fig. 61) opposite Sant'Agostino has been designated by a marble tablet as that of Andrea Sansovino. Tradition identifies it as that house which Andrea built for himself in his native village.[22] It probably dates from about 1516, the year of his marriage. There are three stories, of which the uppermost is separated from the others by a stringcourse. Besides the triple horizontal division the façade is divided into three sections vertically, like the façade of a Venetian house, by a central massing of large windows in the two upper stories. The windows have remarkably broad stone frames, with no mouldings at all or very simple ones. The central windows of the principal floor are accented by broad, flat, scroll-like keystones. With the exception of the eccentric Tuscan arch of the doorway, all of the lines of the house are vertical or horizontal — the horizontal predominating — and tend to give a rather stiff, geometrical effect to the design.

Also, Vasari informs us, Andrea built another dwelling house for the astrologer Pietro Geri, in Arezzo. The house, which later belonged to the anatomist Andrea Cesalpino, was said to be a simple one without architectural interest.[23]

The cloister of Sant'Agostino (Fig. 62) (designed in 1523 and executed ten years later by Domenico di Nanni and his son [24]) is the most interesting and most characteristic piece of architecture by Sansovino. He attempted to build a colonnade that should have the appearance of being symmetrical, around a quadrilateral area with sides of four different lengths. He did this in order to use existing foundations, but one may be sure that Sansovino welcomed the opportunity to display his ingenuity.[25] Each side of the court has four arches, but they vary in width as much as fourteen inches. The corner piers are large and L-shaped, with unequal arms so designed as to disguise the irregular angle. The columns on the ground floor are Doric ($76\frac{3}{4}$ inches high), rest on a low parapet, and bear arches which come down directly on the capitals. The Ionic columns of the upper level are spaced to come directly over the Doric columns below. They are on a low parapet also, and support timber beams. The capitals have four separate volutes of a simple, loosely rolled type, which are superposed over Roman Doric echini. Two stringcourses mark the floor level between the stories, and give the unusual emphasis to the horizontal which Sansovino liked.

Designed at the same time by Sansovino and carried out by Domenico di Nanni were the pulpit and singing gallery of the adjacent church. The pulpit has been destroyed and replaced by one of later design. The gallery, however, remains. It is in the form of a little balcony supported by Ionic columns (Fig. 63), and occupies the west end of the church. The columns of the lower level are exquisitely precise in design and carving. They support low architrave blocks from which arches spring to support groin vaults. The order on the upper level piers is most peculiar. Indeed, one doubts whether it should be called an order; there are no mouldings in relief, what seem to be volutes are mere lateral bulges, and the proportions are thoroughly unorthodox.

The Doric portal (Fig. 64), which is now the street entrance to the chapel of San Giovanni Battista, adjoining Sant'Agostino, is most pleasing in design and proportions. Like the rest of Sansovino's architecture at Monte San Savino it is built of a local variation of *pietra serena*, which carves easily and has a handsome appearance, but weathers poorly. Consequently the restoration of the doorway a few years ago almost meant replacement. The work, however, was well done, and the result is happy. Here Sansovino was able to keep the columns and entablature light by setting the columns on pedestals. Otherwise, columns which were equal in height to the door would have demanded an over-heavy entablature. At the same time he avoided the weak effect of too thin columns by placing in back of them pilasters which project to the sides. The result is one of lightness and elegance combined with breadth and stability.

Opposite the Palazzo Ciocchi del Monte is a graceful open loggia, the not infrequent attribute of a Tuscan palace. Stegmann [26] attributed it rightly to Andrea Sansovino, although a ninety-year old tradition ascribes it to Antonio da San Gallo the Elder, who was the author of the palace which faces it.

The main façade (Fig. 65) is composed of five arches resting on two terminal piers and four intermediate Corinthian columns, reminding one forcibly of those on the Santa Casa (Fig. 49), which Sansovino probably took as models for these. The archivolts are carved with architrave mouldings and rest on architrave blocks. In the spandrels are the "mountains" of the Ciocchi arms, enclosed in delicately carved laurel wreaths. Above come a frieze band and a cornice. Between the cornice and the eaves is a low attic pierced by rounded oblong windows with scroll frames. The corner piers are decorated with Corinthian pilasters.

The broad space under the arcade (Fig. 66) has a flat, vaulted ceiling (recently restored), and walls with pilasters which continue the order of the exterior. There are three doorways on the long wall and a larger, blind portal at one end. The necking moulding of the columns and the cornice moulding of the doors are carried around the three walls. Sansovino's insistence on the horizontal is unusually pronounced here. Below the architrave band in the second and fourth bays of the long wall are little oval windows with curious ornate frames, carved with honeysuckles and volutes.

The part of the structure into which the doors lead has no architectural interest inside or out except in the back, where the basement wall is beautifully rusticated.

Stegmann [27] also rightfully attributed to Andrea yet another bit of architecture in Monte San Savino. It is the courtyard of the former dormitory of Santa Chiara on the Piazza Gamurrini. The present condition of the once elegant little court is deplorable, but Stegmann's engravings permit one to place it high in Sansovino's architectural achievements.

In 1524 Sansovino furnished a design for the steps in front of the cathedral of Arezzo.[28] Evidently the design carried out was that of Guillaume de Marcillat,[29] the famous glass painter who was the first master of Vasari.

In 1528 he received another commission from Arezzo to design the chapel of the Madonna delle Lagrime in the church of the Santissima Annunziata.[30] This also was not carried into execution, perhaps because of his death in the following year.

VII

THE DRAWINGS OF SANSOVINO

SCULPTORS' drawings from the fifteenth century are rare; still, three of the seven designs of Sansovino that are acceptable attributions may possibly date from the *quattrocento*. Those drawings which contain figures have recently been analyzed so ably and thoroughly by Dr. Middeldorf [1] that I can do little more than summarize his finds.

One is a bit surprised to find such a pictorial sketch as the *St. Joseph in a Landscape* [2] (Fig. 67) from the hand of a sculptor. The explanation is to be found in the early training of Andrea in the Pollajuolo shop. From Antonio Pollajuolo derive the admirable landscape, the succession of pleated folds on the lap of Joseph, and the bony, misshapen feet. The peculiarities of a sculptor's drawing appear in the decisive outlines of solid objects; in the strong plastic modeling, especially of rounded objects; and in the utter disregard of a consistent source of lighting. The head is closely related to that of St. Romuald on the Madonna altar in Monte San Savino (Fig. 2). Because of this, and because of the affinities with the paintings of the Pollajuolo, Dr. Middeldorf believes it to be a very early work of Sansovino. I am not convinced that it is so early, and I find that the head also resembles those of the predella saints (Fig. 19) on the other altar at Monte San Savino, which I believe is posterior to the Corbinelli altar; I find, too, that the type is in close accord with the *St. Anthony* (Fig. 34) in Lucca. My conclusion that the drawing is of later date is fortified by a study of the companion sketch of *Astronomy* [3] (Fig. 68), which is in the same technique (black pencil) on the same kind of white paper. In this, the facial features are beginning to resemble those of the Virtues (Fig. 43) in Santa Maria del Popolo. The liberties taken with the rules of perspective are no indication of an early date, for this ultra-modern tendency to disregard the laws of optics is present in Sansovino's works, even those of monumental import, throughout his life.

It is impossible to suggest any practical purpose for which the sculptor may have done these two drawings that differ so widely in subject matter. The execution of the *Astronomy* may be accounted for by his hobby of cosmography.[4]

Dr. Middeldorf also discovered a design for an altar of the *quattrocento* type in Munich (No. 18670). This drawing (Fig. 69) in pen and ink he believes to be a preliminary study for the Corbinelli altar because of the unusual occurrence of a predella relief of the Last Supper. The angels bearing candelabra resemble those in the lunettes of the two Santa Chiara altars (Figs. 2 and 18); the seated saints are related to the figure of Joseph in the drawing mentioned above; and the Virtues are forerunners of the well-known figures of the Santa Maria del Popolo tombs.

Dr. Middeldorf argues that this cannot be a design for the altar that Sansovino made a model of in 1504 for the Duomo, because of the unlikelihood that an artist of such originality would revert to a type that was out of style. On the other hand, the outlines of the small standing saints are surprisingly *cinquecento* in effect. The style of the architecture is little evidence for an early date, since it is quite in accord with the courtyard at Jesi, and with the architecture of the drawing which is inscribed "Battisterio per la cha. di Loreto" (Fig. 73). In a recent article[5] on the preliminary designs for the Popolo tombs, Dr. Middeldorf has recognized that Andrea continued to design such old-fashioned monuments at least as late as 1505. It is quite possible that this sketch represents one of Sansovino's early

designs for the altar of the Duomo, much the same as the suc-
ceeding drawings are studies for the Popolo tombs.

The very great value of drawings for the understanding of an
artist's work is well brought out in Dr. Middeldorf's most
recent discovery of three designs for tombs by Andrea.[6] He
demonstrates that the first (Fig. 72) is a preliminary study for
the tombs of Santa Maria del Popolo. It has several features,
which were popular in the *quattrocento*, which the artist discarded
in the final design, for example the cassone type of bier, the
round-headed attic, the overflowing of the cloud *motif* in the
tondo of the Madonna and Child, the pilasters without capitals,
and the type of arabesque. On the other hand, the study avoids
certain faults of the marble tombs, such as the placing of the
epitaphic tablet too low, and the overloading of the cornice with
the unnecessary figures of the two angels and God the Father.
Perhaps this last weakness may be laid to the obstinacy of the patron: Browning's *The Bishop Orders his Tomb at St. Praxed's
Church* is not without foundation in fact. The figures of the
Virtues on the drawing are patently early studies for the standing
figures on both tombs. The position of the effigy and the relief
of the Madonna and Child are paralleled on the Basso tomb,
while the shape of the escutcheon is closer to that of the Sforza
tomb. This mixture of the peculiarities of both monuments is
further proof for Dr. Middeldorf's theory that the two tombs in
the choir of Santa Maria del Popolo were part of one original
project and not two successive commissions. He found evidence
for his opinion in the way the epitaph is carved on the Basso
tomb.

The second tomb drawing (Fig. 71) is another preliminary
study for the Popolo monuments. Here the bier is dispensed
with, and the effigy of a cardinal rests directly upon a sarcophagus of the cassone type. This is decorated with floral swags,

bands covered with a *guilloche* pattern, and what appears to be fluting like that on the present tombs. The base on which the sarcophagus stands is adorned with the same arabesque ornamentation as that used on the upper frieze of the Sforza tomb. The wall behind the effigy is divided into three simple panels. The lunette is similar to that of the previous sketch. In the two drawings and in the tombs the *motifs* of the central arch persist. There are always the *tondo* of the Madonna and Child, the cherubim heads, and the prelate asleep above an ornate sarcophagus. Sansovino was uncertain only in the enframement of this niche. In the study now under consideration he proposed to set the central arch over a base (as in the other design) and to enclose it with two arabesqued pilasters supporting a pediment. The podia of the pilasters were to be carved with the arms of the cardinal. Apparently these podia, like those of the Cardinal de Castro (died 1506) in Santa Maria del Popolo, were to project about their own width, so that they might carry statues of Saints Peter and Paul. These statues, two-thirds life size, would stand in front of the pilasters much the same as do the boys on the Marsuppini tomb by Desiderio da Settignano.

The St. Peter recalls the St. Matthew of the Corbinelli altar both in pose and type. His keys are enormous. The St. Paul, with a sword in his outstretched hand, is a fiery old soldier (is this an allusion to Julius II?) in contrast to the dreamy, reflective Peter. The St. Paul belongs to the family of Andrea's Baptists and the *St. Anthony Abbot* at Lucca.

The *genii* of the spandrels, who bear attenuated and elongated cornucopias, are rough studies for those executed on the tombs. These active, youthful male figures which Andrea was ever using in the spandrels, as well as those on the beautiful acanthus panel of the Basso tomb (Fig. 42), vividly recall the lithe yet muscular figures of Antonio Pollajuolo. In general, however, these are more graceful, and more posed. Now these qualities are precisely what mark off the bronze statuettes of *Hercules* (Kaiser Friederich Museum, Berlin) and of *David* (formerly in the Morgan collection, New York) from the authentic work of Pollajuolo. Is it possible that the statuettes are by Sansovino?

Sansovino took drastic liberties with the entablature: the frieze and all the ornamented mouldings of the cornice are suppressed. If this was done for the sake of compactness — to keep the tomb low — it presents a great contrast with the finished tombs, which are too high. The tympanum of the pediment is decorated with the Rovere shield under the papal insignia, an oak wreath, and sinuous streamers. At the sides are two candelabra on pedestals that continue the lines of the pilasters. As on the carved tombs, great leaf-scrolls are used as acroteria. The crowning feature of the attic is an ornate cross flory which stands on a scroll-flanked base.

The third sepulchral design (Fig. 74) appears to have been made in an attempt to secure the commission for the tomb of Leo X. Apparently Leo did not plan any monument for himself, so it is logical to suppose that this was made to submit to Pope Clement VII. That would make this drawing date as late as 1523. The figures remind one very much of those on the tombs in Santa Maria del Popolo. Apropos of what I have said about the probability of a later date for some works (especially the St. Lawrence altar and the two pencil drawings), observe the draughtsmanship and proportions of the two seated Virtues.

Dr. Middeldorf suggests that the architectural portion of this design came from the collaboration of one of the greater architects. This is, indeed, a compliment to Sansovino, for a close study of his Doric portal and the singing gallery in Monte San Savino reveals precisely the same feeling for architectural design and detail that appear here. On the other hand, there is no doubt that in his later architectural designs Andrea was much influenced not only by Bramante but also by the younger architects Peruzzi, Raphael, and Antonio da San Gallo the Younger.

The only purely architectural drawing which I assign to Sansovino is inscribed "Sansovino — Battisterio per la cha. di Loreto" (Fig. 73), in a handwriting at least as late as 1550. It would, in truth, be a curious project for a baptistry, and I am inclined to think that it may have been a study for a building in the background of a picture or pictorial relief.[7] The study is executed in pen and wash with black ink used for the lines and a light cool brown wash for shadows on paper which has turned brownish. It is drawing No. 20 in the section of architectural drawings of the Uffizi collection.

In the Palazzo Comunale of Monte San Savino is a folio sheet, written on both sides in the sculptor's handwriting, with some details of hydraulics, an account of his invention of a geometrical instrument (a sort of astrolabe), and a rough sketch of a Doric temple. A further indication of his interest in mechanics is found in an eighteenth-century mention [8] of a sketch inscribed "una sega posto sull'acqua ch'egli fece nel Portogallo per segare uno quadro di diaspro, ma con poco buon esito."

There are in the Uffizi several drawings which have been associated with Sansovino.[9] No. 21 contains two sketches of temples; the character of No. 2 is described by its antique label, "Modo del Sansovino per fortificare la copula delloreto, overo li pilastri della copula"; Nos. 139 and 141, bear an old inscription, "di S. Gallo, il giovane, il quale li eseguiva secondo il modo o concetto del Sansovino." (These show various ways of building classic supports under the Gothic arches of the crossing at Loreto in order to fortify the piers.) Drawing No. 142 is a design for a tomb somewhat similar to those in Santa Maria del Popolo. It appears to be a *pasticcio* of Sansovino *motifs*. Certainly the delineation is not by his hand. In the catalogue of the Uffizi collection of drawings (No. 4703) under the heading of "Altari" is the following notice: "prospetto per un altare — detto da And. Sansovino — Ancona." It does not seem to be by Andrea.

VIII

CONCLUSION

No OTHER artist — except, perhaps, Giovanni Bellini — illustrates so well the transition from the Early to the High Renaissance as Andrea Sansovino. In his predilection for doing statues in relief, rather than in the round, he was still of the *quattrocento*. He never outgrew a certain delight in including flowers, animals, and architecture in pictorial settings. The kind of arabesque he employed is natural and organic in construction. The drapery that he used in nearly all of his work is of that heavy woolen kind which came into Italian art from the Gothic sculpture of the North. He did not believe in art for art's sake like the fully developed artist of the *cinquecento*, but studied with the greatest care the nature of the subject he was depicting, and used all of his knowledge of gesture and facial expression to characterize the figures and to tell the story in the clearest, most effective way. Also most of his figures show a delicacy of limb and a slightness of form that is in strong contrast with the robustness of the sixteenth century.

Florentine artists of the fifteenth century were making scientific discoveries in the field of naturalistic representation. Oftentimes this creeps into their art so that we find realism in details and a lack of naturalism in a work as a whole. Or, again, they were so delighted with their new-found ability to depict objects correctly that they filled their panels with inconsequential paraphernalia, often of interest but always detracting from the total unity. The greatest artists, for example Masaccio, Jacopo della Quercia, Piero dei Franceschi, and Botticelli, avoided this. Botticelli often employed much rich decoration, to be sure, but always he kept it subservient, so that its use enhanced rather than detracted from the main theme. That is true, likewise, of the work of the mature Andrea Sansovino. Even in the Popolo tombs — one must not base judgments upon elevation drawings or upon photographs — the essential unity is so great that the rich decorative *motifs* are secondary to the meaning of the chief figures. This "grand style" which was admired so universally until the end of the past century is a bit too sumptuous for most modern tastes. Would Michelangelo enjoy present favor if his plastic monuments were complete in all their opulence of architectural and figure decoration? I think not. Few are the people who like the ceiling of the Sistine chapel as a ceiling decoration, or the tomb of Julius II in San Pietro in Vincoli as a tomb. While it would be a great loss to art historians, it would be a boon to the reputation of Sansovino were the statues of the Popolo tomb wrenched from their settings and placed in different museums. Such is the caprice of changing fashions.

Sansovino was influenced by antique art — the Temperance (Fig. 44) in Santa Maria del Popolo and the Saint Anne group show that — but much less than is generally thought. Even when he is most classic he is often closer to the art of Andrea Pisano and Arnolfo di Cambio than to the art of Rome. Perhaps the most classic head he ever did is the head of the Virgin in Sant' Agostino (Fig. 48), yet when it is compared simultaneously with antique heads and with the head of the *Beatrice* in Palermo by Francesco Laurana one discovers, with some surprise, that it is much closer to the *quattrocento* work.

Sansovino, like the artists of the previous generation, had a thorough knowledge of facial expression and physical anatomy, but unlike those artists he was able to subordinate this scientific knowledge, since it was no overwhelming novelty to him, to higher artistic purposes. The St. Anne group (Fig. 47) is once again the best illustration of this ability, although the terracotta Virgin and Child of the Bargello (Fig. 27) illustrates it well.

There are no pagan subjects in the *opus* of Sansovino unless one accepts the recently attributed reliefs at Poggio a Cajano. There are, however, decorative masks and figures of pagan derivation in the architectural carving of his tombs, and some of his Christian figures — like some of Raphael's — have more than a slight resemblance to certain antique gods. The Virtues (Figs. 39, 40, 43, 44) of the Popolo monuments have a strong superficial classicism about them, yet they are, without any doubt, merely the final development of the series of Virtues of *quattrocento* Florence. The superiority of Sansovino's productions is undeniable.

It is sometimes said that the artists of the High Renaissance were bound by the tenets of naturalism far more than their "primitive" predecessors. Perhaps so; but one must not forget that the conventions which they adopted have become so much a part of our mode of perception that we do not credit the artists who invented them with originality. Especially is this the case with Raphael, but it is also true of Sansovino, and he who is seeking to appreciate the art of the High Renaissance must remember this, and freshen his eyes to see things as the contemporaries of these artists saw them. Then only will he find full delight in the greatest art of the Renaissance.

APPENDICES

APPENDICES

APPENDIX I

CHRONOLOGY OF THE LIFE OF ANDREA SANSOVINO

1460. Andrea di Nicolò di Domenico di Muccio was probably born in this year at Monte San Savino.[1]

1475–1480. About this time Andrea was working in the shop of Antonio Pollajuolo, and we have notice of a lost drawing of the *Flagellation of Christ* which he did there for his benefactor, Simone Vespucci.[2]

1480–1485. Perhaps during these years he did the terra-cotta plaques of the Roman emperors Nero and Galba. Both were for the house of Simone Vespucci, but Vasari got possession of the *Galba* and took it to Arezzo; the *Nero* is lost.[3] While still strongly under the influence of Pollajuolo, Andrea executed the altar of the Madonna and saints for Sant'Agatha, Monte San Savino (now in Santa Chiara), and the tabernacle in Santa Margherita in Montici. Toward 1485 Sansovino may have modeled the terra-cotta frieze on the villa of Poggio a Caiano which Giuliano da San Gallo was building.[4]

1485, Dec. 13. The Corbinelli family petitioned for the altar of the sacrament in the new church of Santo Spirito, an honor which they had held in the former church that had burned. The petition was granted.[5] It is likely that Sansovino was given the commission to execute the altar soon afterwards.

1485–1500. Works besides the Corbinelli altar which probably belong within this period are: a drawing in Munich which may be a study for the above altar,[6] the pencil drawings of *St. Joseph* and *Astronomy* in the Uffizi,[7] and the terra-cotta altar with Saints Lawrence, Sebastian, and Roch in Santa Chiara, Monte San Savino.

1490, Dec. In the account books of the chapter of Santo Spirito, Andrea di Nicolò received 45 lire and 10 soldi for an unspecified service.[8] This payment may have been for models of capitals for the sacristy, or for the design of the vestibule of the sacristy.

1491, Jan. 5. He was a member of the commission to judge projects for finishing the façade of the cathedral.[9]

1491, Feb. 13. He became a member of the Maestri di pietra e legname.[10]

1491–1493. Lorenzo the Magnificent sent him to Portugal at the request of King John II.[11]

1493–1496. Sansovino was back in Florence working for the baptistry of San Giovanni.[12]

1496–1501. Sansovino returned to Portugal to work for King Emmanuel.[13]

1501–1504. To this period it is likely that the following works belong: the terra-cotta *Madonna and Child* in the Bargello, which formerly belonged to the Etruscologist G. F. Gamurrini of Arezzo and Monte San Savino; the baked clay head in Montepulciano, which is identified as a fragment of a large figure of *King Porsena* mentioned by Vasari; [14] and the wooden statue of *St. Anthony Abbot* in Sant'Andrea, Lucca.

1502, Apr. 28. The Arte de' Mercanti debated giving the commission of two marble statues of *St. John Baptizing Christ* to Sansovino, who had proposed the replacement of a medieval group of the same subject. The next day the commission was given.[15]

1502, June 9. The council of Volterra voted to pay Andrea 30 florins for a baptismal font which he was to do for them.[16]

1502, June 10. Sansovino was given the commission to do a figure in marble of the *Holy Saviour* for the great council hall of the Palazzo Vecchio.[17]

1504, Jan. 13. Sansovino received a permit from the Balía to send the two statues of *John the Baptist* and the *Madonna* to Genoa.[18]

1504, Jan. 25. Vasari relates that Sansovino was on the committee to select a location for the *David* of Michelangelo.[19] Fabriczy maintains that this was impossible because Sansovino was in Genoa.[20]

1504, Dec. 30. He was commissioned to do a marble altar of the Host for the cathedral.[21]

1505, Jan. 18. He was paid 42 lire for a wooden model of the above altar.[22]

1505, Jan. 31. The consuls of the Arte de' Mercanti decided to engage Sansovino to finish the group of the *Baptism of Christ* which he had begun for the baptistry, on condition that he complete the work in ten months. The pay was 50 florins, payable 5 each month.[23]

1505, Jan. 31. He engaged a house for three years in the parish of Santa Maria in Campo.[24]

1505, May 8. Sansovino lent 30 florins to the "Compagnia di M. Vergine, altrimenti de' Bianchi" of Monte San Savino.[25]

1505, May 28. Ascanio Sforza died.

1505, Oct. 16. Julius II issued a letter of safe-conduct for Sansovino to go to Liguria.[26]

1505, Dec. 6. Sansovino closed a contract in Spezia with the shipowner, Bart. Ventura, to transport from twenty-five to thirty cargoes of marble from Avenza, the port of Carrara, to Rome.[27]

1505, Dec. 28. Julius sent Sansovino a letter of safe-conduct for the marble.[28]

1506. It is said that in this year Giuliano da San Gallo made the designs for the façade of Santa Maria dell'Anima,[29] and it is likely that Andrea did the pedimental group for it at this time.

1507. Girolamo Basso della Rovere died.

1508, Apr. 4. Nicolò di Domenico made his will, and divided his property between his sons Andrea and Pietro.[30]

1509, June 3. Francesco Albertini finished his guide of Rome; in it he mentioned the tombs of the Cardinals Sforza and Basso as *in situ*.[31]

1511. In this year, or soon after, was done the round relief portrait of Cardinal Antonio Ciocchi del Monte. The Berlin museum acquired it from the former palace of the family at Monte San Savino.[32]

1512. In this year Sansovino made the group of *St. Anne, the Virgin, and Child* in Sant'Agostino for Johann Goritz.[33]

1512, June 28. The Operai of Santa Maria del Fiore allotted Sansovino, who was absent from Florence, the commission for the Apostles Thaddeus and Matthew.[34] He did not do them.

1513, June 22. Leo X issued a brief making Andrea Sansovino "Capo e Maestro generale della fabbrica Loretana e dell' opera di scultura per l'ornamento della Santa Casa," in place of Giancristoforo Romano, who had died in 1512.[35]

1513, Aug. 16. Leo X authorized the cutting of wood in the communal and private groves in order to facilitate building operations at Loreto. Two similar decrees were issued a year later.[36]

1514, Feb. 6. First proof of Sansovino's presence at Loreto.[37]

1514, May 3. The first marble for the ornamentation of the Santa Casa arrived at Loreto.[38]

1514. Sansovino erected a supporting wall for the dome of the church at Loreto.[39]

1514–1516. The construction of walls, vaults, windows, doorways, and three piers of the Palazzo Canonico was paid for by order of Sansovino.[40]

1515. Sansovino designed a timber bridge over the Musone, a river just north of Loreto.[41]

1515, Jan. 15. The Santa Casa paid Andrea almost four months salary and also for five days at Carrara and twenty at Rome. After this his resident salary was paid regularly until July 2, 1516.[42]

1515, May 1. Sansovino contracted for one hundred thousand bricks.[43]

1515, October. Leo X authorized the acquisition of land, by confiscation if necessary, for the site of the Palazzo Canonico at Loreto. On October 1, 1516, the transaction was completed with Sansovino representing the Santa Casa.[44]

1516 (?). Sansovino submitted a design for the façade of S. Lorenzo in Florence.[45]

1516, Feb. 16. The Santa Casa contracted for four hundred thousand tiles.[46]

1516, July 14. Andrea appears in a contract at Monte San Savino. On September 9 he bought some land there.[47]

1516, Oct. 30. The dowry contract for Andrea's marriage to Marietta di Giovanni Battista Veltroni was signed.[48]

1517. Sansovino was in residence at Loreto except from June 17 to October 1.[49]

1517. An expedition went to Dalmatia to quarry stone for Loreto. In 1520 another expedition was sent to convey it to Loreto.[50]

1517, Jan. 13. Sansovino acted as a witness at Loreto.[51]

1517, Jan. 17. Leo X sent Sansovino a brief of authority to cut saplings and bushes wherever he wished.[52]

1517, Jan. 18. Leo X charged Antonio da San Gallo the Younger to make a complete inspection of the works at Loreto.[53]

1517, June. Between this time and November 21, 1517, Simone Resse succeeded Sansovino as architect at Loreto. Sansovino retained charge of all the sculptural work.[54]

1517, or later. The loggia opposite the Palazzo Ciocchi at Monte San Savino is later than 1517, according to a manuscript in the palace.[55] About this time Sansovino must have designed his own house at Monte San Savino, the former dormitory connected with Santa Chiara at Monte San Savino, and the house of the astrologer Pietro Geri at Arezzo.[56]

1518. Sansovino was in residence at Loreto except from July to September.[57]

1518, Sept. 21. Andrea is cited in the *rogiti* of Monte San Savino on this day, and again on December 18.[58]

1518, Nov. 23. Between this date and July 15, 1520, Sansovino received five payments on account for the reliefs which he was making for the Santa Casa. The first payment was made in Rome.[59]

1519, July. He designed the courtyard of the Palazzo del Comune at Jesi.[60]

1519, July 10. Sansovino's monthly stipend of 15 ducats was suspended.[61]

1519, Aug. 22. Andrea appears in the *rogiti* of Monte San Savino on this date, and again on September 1 and 6, October 29, and November 1.[62]

1520–1526. Large payments were made for the construction of the palace at Loreto. Bartolomeo da Forlì and Silvestro da S. Guisto decorated several of the rooms.[63]

1520, Jan. 30. Sansovino received 20 ducats for the previous two and a half months. Cardinal Bibiena ordered that the sculptor's salary be suspended in the future.[64]

1520, Sept. 21. Sansovino is cited in the *rogiti* of Monte San Savino, and again on October 1.[65]

1520, Dec. 20. Leo X sent a brief confirming Sansovino's status as master of sculpture for the Santa Casa. His salary was set at 10 ducats a month.[66]

1521, Jan. 1. Sansovino received 100 ducats for a half of the relief of the *Annunciation* and a half of the *Adoration of the Shepherds*. He also received a large indemnity for his unpaid salary and expenses.[67]

1521, Jan. 20. The prior of Capua wrote the governor of Loreto the conditions of Sansovino's new status.[68]

1521, June 24. Andrea was paid 166⅔ ducats for beginning a new *storia* for the Santa Casa.[69]

1521. Sansovino designed towers for the walls of the city of Jesi.[70]

1522, April 17. Sansovino left Loreto. He returned for the months of May and June, and then was absent for a long time.[71]

1522, June 19. Andrea was paid 166⅔ ducats for the *storia* which he was making and for the *quadro* which he had finished that day.[72]

1522, October. Andrea was busy buying land at Monte San Savino.[73]

1523, March 28. Andrea returned to Loreto after an absence of nine months. He stayed little more than a month.[74]

1523. Date on the lintel of Santa Maria in Porta Paradisi, Rome.

1523, April 12. Sansovino is cited in the *rogiti* of Monte San Savino, and again on May 27.[75]

1523, July 1. Andrea left Loreto to go to Monte San Savino. It appears he did not return before December.[76]

1523. Andrea designed the singing gallery and pulpit (the latter is not extant) for Sant'Agostino in Monte San Savino, and also the adjoining cloister. These designs were carried out ten years later by Domenico di Nanni and his son. For the Compagnia di Santo Antonio he did a Doric portal in this cloister. It is now the entrance to San Giovanni.[77]

1523, July 26. Sansovino's name appears in the *rogiti* of Monte San Savino on this date, and on August 28, November 26, December 7, and December 18.[78]

1523, Dec. 23. Clement VII reappointed Sansovino master of the works at Loreto. He had charge of both sculpture and architecture.[79]

1524, Jan. 1. Sansovino at Loreto wrote to Michelangelo asking to be taken on as an assistant (for the work on the Biblioteca Laurenziana and the Medici chapel). Clement VII suggested the idea to Andrea. Since Michelangelo did not reply, Sansovino wrote again on March 2 and December 5.[80]

1524, May 30. Sansovino turned over to the authorities of the Santa Casa the two tablets of marble which he had finished carving. The reliefs of the *Annunciation* and the *Adoration of the Shepherds* were complete. Andrea left Loreto for fear of the plague.[81]

1524, June 10. In this year Sansovino's name appears in the *rogiti* of his native village on June 10, August 25, September 21, and November 13.[82]

1524. Andrea furnished a design for the steps in front of the cathedral of Arezzo.[83]

1525, May 29. Andrea was paid for twenty-one days residence at Loreto, then departed.[84]

1525, June 22. From this date to August 31 Sansovino was at Loreto.[85]

1526, June 30. Sansovino left Loreto after six months in residence there.[86]

1527. Andrea's name is cited in the *rogiti* of Monte San Savino on January 2, January 6, January 8, January 19, January 20, February 17, March 4, March 10, and March 24.[87]

1527, May 27. The Santa Casa paid Sansovino's son, Camillo, 20 ducats, which were charged to Andrea's account against the *storia* which he was making.[88]

1527, June 24. Sansovino received 166⅔ ducats as the first third payment on the *storia* (the *Marriage*) which he was making. One half was almost finished.[89]

1527, June 29. Sansovino left Loreto for good, after having been there most of the time since the first of the year.[90] During the following period of retirement he must have modeled the terra-cotta *Saint Roch* for the church of San Quirico in Battifolle.[91]

1528, June 28. Sansovino is mentioned in the *rogiti* of Monte San Savino, and again on August 15.[92]

1528, Sept. 29. He was called to design the chapel of the Madonna delle Lagrime in SS. Annunziata at Arezzo.[93] This was not carried out.

1529. Sansovino died in Monte San Savino,[94] some time after March 2.[95]

APPENDIX II

DOCUMENT I

Archivio Nazionale, Firenze: Libro Nero Determinazione, vol. A, da 1440 a 1554, Convento 122, vol. 27 @ 138.[1]

Questa e una copia di una scripta fatta alla chasa de corbinegli quando demo loro el corpo di cristo.

Anno domini Mcccclxxxv, die xiii decembris.

Sia noto questo manifesto a ciaschuno come ragunati e padri reverendi maestri e gli altri padri et frati del convento di santo spirito di firenze dell'ordine de frati heremitani di santo agostino per comandamento del reverendo padre magistro michele da empoli priore del sopra detto convento a suono di camponella come e usanza di ragunare detto capitolo fu ora posto da el sopra detto reverendo priore a detti reverendi maestri e padri come essendo ricaschato al convento el dare del luogo del santissimo corpo di cristo per rispetto dell'arsione della chiesa vechia, e a dimandati e detti reverendi maestri e padri se alcuno vi fussi che ad alcuna nobile casa per comune consenso o per scriptura fusse dato rispose ciascheduno nel suo luogo, cio di detta arsione nunquam non esser stato publicamente di comune consenso dato et chi nella vechia chiesa l'aveva avendo ceduto et non ripiglando et essendo dalla generosa chasa de corbinegli a domandato a dimando el sopra detto reverendo priore ciascheduno privatamente se era contento che detto sacratissimo sacramento del corpo di cristo si concedessi donissi et liberamente si langissi alla detta generosa et nobile casa di corbinegli et cosi ciascheduno privatamente a voce viva rispose del si et cosi fu nel sopra detto di concesso el detto sacramento a detta chasa conquesto che detta chasa tenghi detto sacramento honorificamente et sempre con lume aceso dinanzi et per la festa del corpo di cristo vi mandino le falcole et cosi el giovedi santo et cosi con quegli ornamenti che meritamente detto sacramento merita et accio che questo sia dato validamente se fatto per inareza [sic] questa scripta e ciascheduno ci porra la sua nome propria qui di sotto anno et di e mese sopra scripto.

Io magistro benedetto da firenze i degno provinciale della pisana che in ora non mi essendo piu — nato [2] a concedenda lori detto sacramento son contento e cosi per mia volonta lo dono alla detta chasa.

Io magistro michele da empoli priore del convento di santo spirito conformo le sopra dette cose.

Io magistro andrea dall'exandria sono contento aquanto di sopra si contiene.

Io magistro Nicholaio da firenze sono contento aquanto di sopra si contiene.

Io frate giovannj di berto padini sapore sono contento aquanto di sopra si contiene.

Io frate costantino baccelliere da prato sono contento aquanto di sopra si contiene.

Io frate sebastiano biblico da firenze sono contento aquanto di sopra si contiene.

Io frate francesco da firenze sono contento aquanto di sopra si contiene.

Io frate lorenzo di francesco da castel francho sono contento aquanto di sopra si contiene.

Io frate iacobo de valentia lectore sono contento quanto di sopra si contiene.

Io frate ypolito da cortona sacrestano sono contento quanto di sopra si contiene.

DOCUMENT II

Archivio Nazionale, Firenze: Convento 122, vol. 128 @ 221[t].[3]

a dj 9 di marzo 1492 [1493 by our calendar] Raghunoronsi gli spettabili Operai in palazzo in chamera del gonfaloniere e chon loro chomesione ordinai vi venise a la loro presenza alquanti maestri intendenti fra quali vi fu Simone del Polaiuo, Giuliano da Sangallo, Giovanni di Betto, Salvi d'Andrea, e Pagno d'Antonio e dal loro vollono parere chome si dovesse fare la volta che sa [si ha a] fare inanza sentri in sagrestia dove sono messe le 12 colone sela [se ella] si facesse di ghiaia o di mattoni o di pietra lavorata, dove dacchordo tutti disono che sendo cominciata riccha e chon tante cholone che la si facesse di pietra di macignio riquadrata e tavolata chon rose o altro che stesse bene dove inteso loro rimasono che Simone e Giuliano fussino con Piero di lorenzo [de' Medici] e mostransegli [sic] qualche disegno e che in lui la rimesono.

DOCUMENT III

Archivio della Santa Casa, Loreto. Strumenti III @ 145r.[4]

Dilecto filio Andreae de S. to Savino superstanti Fabricae S. Mariae de Laureto.

Leo pp. X

Dilecte fili salut. et apostolicam Benedictionem. Cupientes ut fabrica templi sive domus beatissimae Mariae semper Virginis de Laureto, quae multis in dies claret miraculis, ad quamque ex remotissimis Orbis partibus christifidelium multitudo devotionis causa confluit, iam magno sumptu caepta continuari, decenterque strui, et iuxta cordis nostri desirium, et eam quam ad eamdem Virginem Mariam devotionem gerimus perfici possit: de tua fide, integritate atque Architecturae et Sculpturae Artium sufficientia plurimum in Domino confisi: ac sperantes quod ea quae tibi duxerimus committenda bene

et laudabiliter exequeris; Te fabricae et operi eiusdem domus sive templi
praeficiendum duximus, et ad nostrum beneplacitum praeficimus per praesentes. Cui rei ut melius intendere possis, laborum et comodorum tuorum
(ut par est) rationem habere volentes, tibi salarium quindecim Ducatorum
auri de Camera pro singulo mense, quamdiu eidem fabricae praefueris, videlicet
pro eisdem mensibus anni quibus ibidem residebis, seu pro rebus eamdem
fabricam concernentibus alibi te esse contigerit, constituimus, ac per Camerar-
ium dictae domus singulis tribus mensibus de pecuniis dictae domus, si quolibet
mense pecuniae paratae non essent, ut praefertur ad eamdem rationem persolvi:
et honestam habitationem pro persona tua, unoque familiari tuo et uno equo:
cum sumptibus victus tam tui, quam familiaris et equi per Gubernatorem
dictae domus sive templi pro tempore existentem tibi assignari volumus et
mandamus. Etiam tibi concedimus quod per quatuor menses quolibet anno
quo volueris pro tuis negotiis libere te conferre et residere possis, cura dictae
fabricae non obmissa, ita tamen quod si contigerit aliqua necessitas dictae
fabricae, etiam durante dicto tempore quatuor mensium, absque mora te illuc
conferre tenearis, et oportune providere. Quo autem tempore absens fueris,
quod quidem tempus ultra quatuor menses (ut praefertur) extendi non volumus, eo tempore singulis quibusque mensibus salarium sex ducatorum auri
de Camera tibi constituimus. Ut autem tibi commissa comodius celeriusque
exequi possis, omnes et singulos magistros tam murorum, quam lignorum, ac
alios operarios pro dicta fabrica necessarios ponendi, et iam positos (si tibi
minus idonei et inutiles videbuntur) amovendi et deponendi, aliosque illorum
loco pro tuo arbitrio subrogandi: marmora aliosque lapides fodi: et ligna omnis
generis incidi faciendi: oportuna aedificia designandi, locandi, struendi, et iam
structa (prout opus fuerit, et tibi videbitur) diruendi et evertendi, nec non
omnia et singula mandandi, praecipiendi, gerendi et exercendi quae in praemissis, et circa ea necessaria fuerint, aut quomodolibet opportuna, plenam et
amplam potestatem et facultatem tibi concedimus per praesentes. Mandantes
eisdem magistris, operariis et caeteris mercenariis, quos tu conduxeris, aliisque
ex iam conductis, qui operi intendunt, ut tibi in praemissis tamquam eorum
praefecto prompte pareant et intendant. In contrarium facientibus non obstantibus quibuscumque. Datum Romae apud S. Petrum sub Anulo Piscatoris, die XXII Junii M. D. XIII, Pontificatus nostri Anno primo.

P. Bembus

DOCUMENT IV

Archivio della Santa Casa, Loreto. Libro Mastro, vol. A, 1514–1516 @ 58. [5]

(1515) M° Andrea dal Monte San Sovino de' avere addì XV de ienaio
fl. LXXXIIII, bl. XXXIII, sono per suo servito de mesi IIII non fatto innordinanza, e dì XXV, scritto innordinanza in salario X, dì V è la gita di Charara,
dì XX Roma.

DOCUMENT V

Archivio della Santa Casa, Loreto. Strumenti III @ 163.[6]

Dilecto filio Andreae de Monte Sti. Savini Architecto Fabricae beatae Mariae
lauretan. praefecto.

LEO PP. X

Dilecte fili salutem et apostolicam Benedictionem. Intelligentes, te pro
lateribus coquendis et calce conficienda pro aedificatione istius templi beate
Mariae lauretanae curae tuae per nos commissi, non modico lignamine in-
digere, Nos ne propterea tam divinum opus retardetur, volumus concedimus-
que tibi, ut ubique per loca vicina fructices et arbusta omnis generis inutilia,
et fructum non facentia ad rem hanc incidi, et quo opus fuerit comportari
facere libere possis: soluto tamen illorum dominis, si particulares personae
fuerint, iusto et convenienti praecio: si vero locorum universitates, iusti
praecii medietate. Mandant. universis et singulis civitatum, terrarum et
locorum Nobis et S. Ro. Ecclesiae subiectorum Comunitatibus et particulari-
bus personis in virtute sanctae obedientiae, ut recepto praecio ut praefertur,
te in eorum agris et iurisdictionibus fructices et arbusta praedicta incidi et
quo volueris comportari facere libere permictant: Officialibus autem nostris
quocumque nomine nuncupentur, ut hac nostra concessione, quoad opus
fuerit, absque ullo impedimento frui omnino faciant. Quibusvis contrariis non
obstantibus. Datum Romae apud S. Petrum sub Annulo Piscatoris, die.
XVII Januarii, M. D. XVII, Pontificatus nostri anno quarto

BEMBUS

DOCUMENT VI

Archivio della Santa Casa, Loreto. Strumenti III @ 162v.[7]

Dilectis filiis Gubernatori domus beatae Mariae de Laureto et Andreae de
Monte S. Savini Fabricae domus Praefecto.

LEO PP. X

Dilecti filii salutem et apostolicam Benedictionem. Quoniam curae nobis
est, ut templum istud beatae Mariae et Domus lauretana quam recte absol-
vantur, mittimus istuc dilectum filium Antonium de Sancto Gallo Archi-
tectum, hominem quidem in construendis aedificiis optimi judicii, cum dilecti
item filii nostri B. Card. S. Mariae in Porticu, eius templi et domus Pro-
tectoris, mandatis: qui aedificationem illam omnem perspiciat, et consideret,
nobisque omnia referat. Mandamus itaque vobis, ut totius operis rationem
illi ostendatis, quo tota de re instructus, id omne nobis denuntiare possit.
Datum Romae, apud S. Petrum, sub Annulo Piscatoris, die XVIII Januarii,
M.D. XVII. Pontificatus nostri Anno quarto.

BEMBUS

DOCUMENT VII

Archivio della Santa Casa, Loreto. Libro Mastro, vol. B, 1517–1518 @ 50 a & b.[8]

E a dì XVIII de giugno [1518?, to maestro Andrea] li ferono lettera ms. Antonio canseliero vicetesauriere a li heredi de Tadeo Gaddi di Firenze che lieli pagassino, f. 210, etc.

Et de' havere [maestro Andrea] ... facti pagari a Baccio de Michelangelo orefice de Firenze scultore da ms. Luigi Gaddi delli duc. 300 in contro, fio. 210.

Et de' havere ... che tanti ne fece pagare a Domenico di Bologna scultore da ms. Luigi Gaddi, fio. 210.

DOCUMENT VIII

Archivio della Santa Casa. Libro Mastro, vol. C, 1518–1520 @ 23.[9]

(1518) M° Andrea da Monte San Savino scultore de' dare a dì 23 di novembre fl. 102, bl. 20, li fa pagare in Roma ms. Cynthio Philonardo in ducati Larghi d'oro di cambera, a conto delle storie ha di fare per la cappella della Madonna Santa Maria de Loreto, fl. 102, bl. 20.

E a dì XII dicembre de' dare duc. cento d'oro di cambera: da ms. Luigi Gaddi thesaurario fl. 205.

E a dì XI di luglio 1519 ducati cento d'oro Larghi a buon conto; et per noi da ms. Luigi Gaddi fl. 210.

E a dì 24 di novembre duc. cento d'oro Largo a buon conto: et per noi da ms. Luigi Gaddi fl. 210.

E a dì 15 di luglio [1520] duc. 150 d'oro, li quali hanno pagati per noi a buon conto li Gaddi di Roma, fl. 315.

maestro Andrea dal monte santo Savino scultore di contro debe havere ducati cinquecento d'oro largo et sono per sua manifactura di dua quatri fatti per l'ornamento della cappella della madona cioe uno quatro della nativita di christo et uno della nuntiata et di tanto e stato ordinato da S. Superiori. Si li facci buoni cioe ducati cinquecento d'oro largo per storia; ogni storia sono dua quatri posto ornamento della cappella in questo @ 175 ducati 1050.

Et debe havere ducati ccxxv bol. 37 den. vxi li quali si li fanno buoni per suo servito del tempo passato; insine a questo dì primo di ganaio 1521 et di questo e la volonta di N. S. papa leone come se visto per una lettera del reverendo signore priore di capua Signor Protectore di questa santissima casa hauto questo dì xxvi di genaro in mano nostro reverendo monsignor gubernator et registrato el breve e la lettera per mano di magister mangiorgio canonico et canciliere della casa posto ornamento in questo — @ 175 ducati 225. 37–16 ducati 1275. 37 . 16

DOCUMENT IX

Archivio della Santa Casa. Strumenti III.[10]

Dilecto filio Andreae Sansovino Sculptori.

Leo pp. X

Dilecte fili s. et a. b. Cum pro immensis atque infinitis in humanum genus ac praecipue in nos ipsos ab immaculata summi Dei redemptoris nostri Genitrice collatis beneficiis, sacrosanctam, totoque terrarum orbe venerandam Lauretanam Ecclesiam, quam eiusdem Virginis carnis sarcinam ferentis cellulam extitisse, et angelicae salutationis atque divini partus, quem aeditura esset, nuncii patuisse, devote ac pie credimus, et in qua se virgo ipsa uberiorem in dies singulos exhibet gratiarum largitricem fidelium cunctorum votis praesto succurens, sub nostra imediata protectione atque administratione susceperimus: proptereaque omnium operum, quae ad ipsius Ecclesiae ac ad aedificiorum continentiam instaurationem ornamentum amplificationem, caepta sunt, perfectionem tota mente cupiamus, unus tu nobis occurris, cui, ob egregiam ac singularem in sculptura atque architectura peritiam, fidem et solertiam huiusque praestitam, cunctorum operum in ipso loco scalpello peragendorum praecipuam curam, ac speciale onus demandemus. Te igitur super ipsis operibus scalpello conficiendis praesentium tenore praeficimus, sive, ut vulgo dicitur, caput magistrum deputamus, tibique ac censurae tuae omnes operarios, ministros seu famulos ad scalpelli exercitium conductos et conducendos subiicimus, cum potestate inertes ac minus inertes removendi, aliosque aptiores in eorundem loco surrogandi, caeteraque agendi quae in similibus archimagistri agere consueverint. Assignantes et constituentes tibi pro huiusmodi oneris mercede salarium decem florenor. auri largor, mense quolibet, kalendis proximis Januarii solutione incipiente: ita ut integro anno summam centum et viginti florenor. similium percipias: hac adiecta conditione, quod tribus mensibus aestivis, vid. a kalendis julii usque ad kalendas octobris propter aeris intemperiem vacare et loco abesse possis, rediturus tamen si te interim ab eiusdem loci agentibus pro ipsorum operum necessitatibus vocari contigerit. Ad quorum quidem decem florenor. rationem pro mensibus quoque decursis, de quibus non est tibi integre satisfactum, satisfieri mandamus. Insuper volumus, ut istoria Virginis Annunciatae et Natalis dominici, quas tuis manibus in marmoream sculpturam redigere caepisti, infra triennium complere, ac perficere tenearis; pro cuiuslibet ipsarum istoriarum mercede florenos auri largos quingentos, tribus vicibus, vid. initio medio et fine earumdem aequabiliter persolvendos, atque ultra nostrae voluntatis et discretionis praemium: nec non domus quam nunc inhabitas usum cum utensilibus in ea existentibus, gratis et sine aliqua solutione pensionis recepturus. Quae omnia per Gubernatores eiusdem loci, seu introituum administratores ibidem deputatos, et alias per quoscumque ad quos spectat sive spectare poterit, plene observari, et tibi de solutionibus praemissis congruis temporibus [provi]deri (?), sola praesentium obstensione absque alia desuper facienda commissione sive mandato, committimus et mandamus: contrariis non obstantibus quibuscumque, praesentibus ad nostrum beneplacitum duraturis. Datum Romae apud S. Petrum sub Annulo Piscatoris, die XX Decembris, M. D. XX, Pontificatus nostri Anno ottavo

IA. SADOLETUS

DOCUMENT X

Archivio della Santa Casa. Strumenti III @ 180.[11]

Al R. do Mons. mio Mons. il Vescovo di Santo Angelo Governatore di Loreto.

R. do Mons. mio, la S. tà di N. S. re vole continuar servirse di M° Andrea dal Monte, et che sia capo maestro dell'opera del scarpello, tanto nello adornamento de la cappella, quanto in ogni altra cosa, dove haverà intervenine lo scarpello, fornisca li doi quadri tiene in mano, et tucto quello che ha hauto dalla Casa sin ad mo', che intendo sono circa secento venti ducati d'oro, siano per pagamento di detta storia. Et vole S. S. tà se gli dia di provisione diece Ducati d'oro il mese, et le storie restan da farsi vole la S. tà S. se li paghino ad ragione di cinquecento ducati la una, la quale cominciata se li dia il terzo di detti cinquecento ducati anticipati, l'altro terzo quando l'harrà mezza facta, et il resto d'il pagamento finita la haverà: et così continuare ogni storia, cominciando l'una poi finita l'altra, pigliando di danari se li anticiperà cautela pubblica, di sorte che in caso di morte non si perdono, et che le storie siano facte di sua mano, et non di altri. La casa dove suole habitare glie resti per servire, pigliando quella obligatione lui vorià dar di se medesmo, al tempo quando darrà la opera, che ha ad esser di sua mano fornita. La presente, di poi de factone pigliar la copia, resti al presentante per sua cautela. Facta in Roma alli 20 di gennaro M. D. XXI.

Al Servitio di V. R. da S.

EL PRIOR DI CAPUA.

DOCUMENT XI

Archivio della Santa Casa. Libro Mastro, vol. D, 1521–1523 @ 6.[12]

maestro Andrea dal monte Santo Savino sta con la casa per scultore et per capo maestro di tucto lo scarpello et debe havere per suo pingione cioe: ducati 10 d'oro largo el mese; chomincia la di sua pingione a dì primo di genaro et non di havere piu la spese: et piu ha davere el dicto maestro Andrea ducati cinquecento d'oro largo per ogni storia che farà per l'ornamento della capella cioe per ogni dua quatri finiti et bene lavorati et fatti di sua mano et li dicti

ducati 500 largo li debe havere; Le paghe; principio mezo 12simo et si che
queste cose li sono ordinato per la santa di N. S. et per reverendo et magnifico
Sor. priore di capua dignissimo prottetore di questa alma casa lavorare fanno
come si insto per breve di sua beatitudine et per lettere di sua S. E.

DOCUMENT XII

Archivio della Santa Casa. Libro Mastro, vol. D, 1521–1523 @ 6.[13]

Et a dì 24 di giugno [1521] duc. 166 et due terzi d'oro Larghi a conto della
Storia che nuovamente fa, hauti per noi dal mag. ms. Luigi Gaddi.

E a dì 19 Junio [1522] duc. 166 et due terzi d'oro Larghi a conto della Storia
che fa, et per un quadro finito questo dì, hauti per noi dal mag. Luigi Gaddi.

DOCUMENT XIII

Archivio della Santa Casa. Libro Mastro, vol. E, 1523 @ 9.[14]

[Andrea del Monte Santo Savino scultore et capo maestro de tutto lo scalpello de questa Alma Casa Laurentana], deve dare, die XIII maii 1523, ducati
undici de oro larghi per sua provisione dalli 28 de marzo che lui retornò, finito
lo ultimo de aprile proximo passato, ad dece ducati el mese: chè luglio, agosto,
septembre, octobre, novembre, decembre, jennaro, febraro, fino a tucti li
27 marzo non ha servito, come trovamo ad libro.

DOCUMENT XIV

Archivio della Santa Casa, Loreto. Libro Mastro, vol. E, 1523 @ 9.[15]

M° Andrea prefato die primo iulii 1523, summo mane, se è partito, et è
andato verso el Monte San Savino: et non se lavora.

DOCUMENT XV

Archivio della Santa Casa, Loreto. Strumenti III @ 186v.[16]

Julianus Rodulphus prior Capuae, Ecclesiae et almae domus lauretan. S. mi
    D. N. Commissarius.

Dilecto nobis in Christo Andreae de Monte Sansavino fabricae et almae
    domus Lauretan. Architectori ac Sculptorum in ea Caput-magistro
    salutem in Domino.

Cum superioribus annis, dum per fae. re. Leonem pp. X, cura et gubernium
almae domus et ecclesiae Lauretan. nobis demandatum esset, fretique probi-

tate et excellentia tua in arte sculptoris provisionem decem ducator. auri de
mandato praefati Leonis fae. re. statuerimus, confiden. quod, quemadmodum
hactenus in his quae ad officium tuum pertinere cognovisti, egregie et laudabiliter te gesseris, de bono in melius continuabis: provisionem praedictam
dictorum decem ducator, auri singulo mense tibi persolvendam ad S. mi D. N.
beneplacitum confirmamus, et quatenus opus sit de novo constituimus et
deputamus. Mandant. locumtenenti nostro moderno et pro tempore existenti
computistae, depositario aliisque officialibus dictae ecclesiae et almae domus
Lauretanae, ad quos in praesens spectat et in futurum spectabit, quatenus
tibi de dicta provisione singulo mense, ad hoc ut comodius te supportare
valeas, integre iñdeant seu iñderi (?) curent cum effectu. Volumus etiam
quod praedicti locumtenens noster, computista, depositarius aliique officiales,
in Architectorem fabricae dictae almae domus et ecclesiae recipiant et admit-
tant, prout nos per presentes te ad tale officium eligimus et deputamus. Contrariis non obstantibus quibuscumque. In quorum omnium et singulorum
fidem ac testimonium praesentes manu nostra propria subscriptas fieri, et per
infrascriptum Cancellarium nostrum subscribi sigillique nostri, quo in similibus utimur, iussimus et fecimus impressione muniri. Datum Romae XXIIII
decembris M. D. XXIII, Pontificatus S. mi D. N. Dmi Clementis VII anno
primo.

Julianus Commissarius ut supra.
AL. RECORDA.

DOCUMENT XVI

Archivio della Santa Casa, Loreto. Libro Mastro, vol. F, 1524–1525 @ 11.[17]

maestro Andrea dal monte san savino scultore et capo maestro della nostra
fabricha debe havere fiorini mille cinquecento tre et bol. xxiiii che tanti si li
fanno buoni questo dì ultimo di maggio cioe ducati cinquecento d'oro larghi
per sua manifactura di dua quatri finiti e consegnateceli in la nostra chiessa
cioe uno della nunptiata e l'altro della nativita di cristo che sono li compagni
delli altri dua quatri factoci che fanno dua storie per l'ornamento della capella
che ogni dua quatri fanno una storia e ogni storia si li pagha ducati cinquecento d'oro larghi come di sopra si dice e il resto sono per la sua provigione di
ducati dieci l'oro simili che li si da ogni messi in nel tempo che sta a Sta. maria
altrimenti no perche non stando dove si lavora non fa el facto della casa la
quale progivione chomincio insine a dì primo di genaro 1521 ordinatoli da
papa leone e e pagato per tucto el presente mese di magio 1524 et si parti per
paura della peste che el pagamento delli dua quatri e della sua provigione
fanno in tucto li ducati 1503 bol. 24 per tucto dicto tempo con lui dacordo
posto ornamento della cappella dare in questo @ 41 ducati 1503.24.

DOCUMENT XVII

Archivio della Santa Casa, Loreto. Libro Mastro, vol. F, 1524–1525 @ 27.[18]

M° Domenicho de Amia da Bologna altramente dicto el Bologna scultore de' dare fior. 756, che de tanti si trova debitore questo dì 4 di genaro a libro paonazo segnato E, 69, et sono per denari datoli a conto della storia che fa per la casa et per il nolo della casa dove habita in Anchona. fl. 756.

E a dì VIIII di Junio 1525, duc. 50 d'oro L. havuti per mano di ms. Juliano Rydolphy in Anchona a conto della storia, che de' finire alla casa, ne' modi et patti che si contiene in nel contracto rogato ser Troylo de Troni de Anchona d. dì. fl. 105.

Mro. Domenicho de Amia da Bologna, altramente dicto el Bologna, scultore, de' havere duc. 552, se li fanno buoni questo dì 5 d'agusto 1525; cioè duc. 500 d'oro L. per conto de'la storia factoci in due quadri, che è la *morte della Madonna*, con l'obbligho come di contra si ve', in l'ultima partita; et duc. 50 simili si li fanno buoni per conto del nolo della casa dove lui ha lavorato la dicta storia; et duc. due pure si li fanno buoni che lui ha dicto havere spesi in fare condurre certi marmi dalla marina alla casa; che tucto fa la somma li duc. 552 d'oro L. Et questo accordo e stato facto dal nostro sig. Locotenente, et mag. ms. Juliano Rydolphy, et ms. Marino Giorgio nostro can. co et cancelliero; et di poi in Anchona facto li contracti con lui d'acordo.

E a dì cinque d'agusto duc. 142 d'oro L. per resto della storia che ci à facto in due quadri et del nolo della casa, computandovi due duc. simili da lui spesi per condurre certi marmi dal mare a casa, et lui si è obbligato havere rata la prima conventione facta con lui come ne appare publico instrumento per mano di ser Troylo de Ancona: pagò ms. Io. bapt.: fl. 298.8

Libro Mastro, vol. F, 1524–1525 @ 41.

E a dì 24 dicto (maggio 1525), fior. 3. bol. 16 spesi in la gita de Anchona per accordare el Bologna scultore per causa non voleva lavorare la storia.

DOCUMENT XVIII

Archivio della Santa Casa. Libro Mastro, vol. G, 1526–1527 @ 41.[19]

(1527) ducati 20 d'oro larghi, li quali si fanno buoni per suo decto al magnif. ms. Luigi Gaddi, che tanti n'hanno pagati li sua di Roma a Camillo, figliolo di dicto m.° Andrea: li quali denari se li mettono a conto della Storia che fa.

E a dì 24 [de iunio], duc. 166 et due terzi d'oro Larghi per la sua terzaria di ducati 500 simili che si li danno per la storia che si fa di due quadri, per ornamento della cappella, che di già si è presso che finito uno, come s'è visto.

DOCUMENT XIX

Archivio della Santa Casa, Loreto. Libro Mastro, vol. K, 1531–1533 @ 9.[20]

maestro Andrea di contro deve haver a dì 11 di octobre 1532 fiorini trecento novanta doj sono per manufactura di una parte de la storia del sposalitio de la madona quale decto maestro in la sua morte lasso imperfetto chome se li fa ad instantia di suoi figlioli ad per stima di maestro Antonio da Sangallo nostro architecto et maestro Ramoi scarpellino da pisia a lornamento in questo @ 11 ducati   392

DOCUMENT XX

Archivio della Santa Casa, Loreto. Libro Mastro, vol. K, 1531–1533 @ 53.[21]

(1533) Nicolo tribolo et con compagni di contro (maestro francesco de Vincenso et maestro Rafaele da montelupo) devono haver a dì 6 di marzo ducati ducento li fa bonj maestro Rafaele da pedeluca scultore sono per la parte sua di ducati 300 degnati dican compagni resta debitrice quando li sera facti bonj li lavorj hanno facto finire questo dì inquesto @ 146 ducati   200

A dì decto ducati ducento li fa boni decto maestro Nicolo tribulo scultore nostro inquesto @ 146 ducati   200

A dì decto ducati ducento li fa boni maestro francesco sangallo scultore nostro inquesto @ 136 ducati   200

A dì prima di octobre ducati sei cento sono per manufactura o ver ed per mita dela historia driamat[ando] la natività de la madona quale havia cominciato maestro Bacio scultore di michelagnolo et hora l'ha finito maestro Rafaele da pedeluca stimato cosi da maestro Antonio Sangallo nostro architecto inquesta @ 188 ducati   600

A dì decto ducati octo cento li fa bonj lornamento dela capella sono per manifactura dele doj storie piccole cioè la visitatione quale ha facto decto maestro rafaele et la presentatione quale ha maestro francesco sangallo inquesto @ 188 ducati   800

A dì decto ducati septocento cinquanta li fa bonj decto ornamento sono per manifactura de la mita dela historia del sposalitio quale ha facto decto maestro Nicolo ad rasione di ducati 750 tucto il quadro come apro e pro contracto rogato maestro alberico nostro archivisto et già canonico inquesto @ 188 ducati   750

A dì decto ducati sei cento facto bonj nts.[?] sono per la manifactura di cinque putini di marmo ad rasione di ducati 35 luno computatione ducat 250 per haver fornito la mita dela historia del sposalitio quale havia lassato imperfecto maestro Andrea sansavino inquesto @ 188 ducati.   600

Summa ducati 3350

NOTES

NOTES

CHAPTER I

[1] Giorgio Vasari, *Opere*, ed. Milanesi, IV (Florence, 1879), 509 ff.

[2] *Idem*, IV, 523.

[3] *Idem.*

[4] See pp. 95 and 100.

[5] Vasari, IV, 509.

[6] C. Frey: "Studien zu Michelagnolo," in *Preuss. Jahrb.*, 1896, pp. 99–101.

[7] Vasari, VI, pp. 142–143.

[8] R. van Marle, *The Italian Schools of Painting*, XI, 364.

[9] Vasari, III, 297.

[10] Van Marle, XI, 387.

[11] Vasari, IV, 510–511.

[12] In *Zeitschrift für bildende Kunst*, 1879, pp. 149–152.

[13] P. Schönfeld, *Andrea Sansovino und seine Schule* (Stuttgart, 1881), p. 5.

[14] In *Preuss. Jahrb.*, 1906, p. 81, note.

[15] U. Middeldorf, "Unknown Drawings of the Two Sansovinos," in *Burlington Magazine*, 1932, pp. 236–245.

[16] C. von Fabriczy, in *Preuss. Jahrb.*, 1906, p. 80 ff.

[17] See Document I.

[18] J. Burckhardt, *Der Cicerone* (Basel, 1855), p. 640.

[19] Schönfeld, p. 8.

[20] A. Marquand, *Giovanni della Robbia* (Princeton, 1920), p. 54.

[21] *Idem*, p. 81.

[22] Jacobus de Voragine, *La Légende Dorée* (edition J.-B. M. Roze) (Paris, 1902), III, 81.

[23] Vasari, IV, 512.

[24] Translated from *La Légende Dorée*, II, 269–271.

[25] In the next chapter I shall adduce evidence to show that Sansovino was in Florence from 1493 to 1496, so that it is possible that this altar was done at that time. The argument for Bertoldo's influence would still be valid, since the changes in Sansovino's style certainly cannot be credited to Portuguese influence.

[26] There are several statues of St. Sebastian which resemble this creation of Sansovino. Notable amongst them are the terra-cotta statuettes of the Victoria and Albert Museum in London (Nos. 7618–1861) and the Kaiser Friederick Museum in Berlin (No. 384). Both of these are to be attributed to assistants. The marble *St. Sebastian* in the left transept of the Cathedral of Como (attributed to Andrea by Biehl) is certainly not by our master. The dry, harsh carving and hard lines are foreign to every period of his sculpture, and details of drapery, hair, and anatomy differ widely from Sansovino's work. The reputed date of this statue, 1499, would be hard to reconcile with Sansovino's chronology.

CHAPTER II

[1] Giorgio Vasari, *Opere*, ed. Milanesi, IV (Florence, 1879), 513–514.

[2] *Idem, Le Vite*, 1st edition (republished by C. Ricci) (Milan and Rome, n. d.).

[3] W. Kallab, *Vasaristudien* (Vienna and Leipzig, 1908), p. 248; C. Frey, *Der literarische Nachlass Giorgio Vasaris* (Munich, 1923), p. 100.

[4] Frey, *idem*, 225, 320.

[5] As we have seen above, Vasari bases the date 1500 on the commencement of the baptistry statues. This is wrong, of course. Nevertheless, Sansovino was probably back in Tuscany in that year.

[6] Vasari, *Le Vite*, ed. C. Frey (Munich, 1911), I, 347.

[7] G. Milanesi, *Giornale Storico degli Archivi Toscani* (Florence, 1860), IV, 66 ff.

[8] Archivio Reale dello Stato di Firenze, Maestri di Pietri e Legname, Libro delle matricole, p. 300.

[9] A. Haupt, *Geschichte der Renaissance in Spanien und Portugal* (Stuttgart, 1927), I, 6.

[10] *Idem*, II, 149.

[11] J. Vasconcellos, "Sansovino," in *Ilustração Moderna*, v (1930), 119.

[12] W. C. Watson, *Portuguese Architecture* (London, 1908), p. 130.

[13] J. Rasteiro, *Quinta e Palacio de Bacalhoa em Azeitão* (Lisbon, 1895), pp. 9–10.

[14] T. Rogge, "Ein Palast Andrea Sansovino's in Portugal," in *Zeitschrift für Bildende Kunst*, N.F., VIII (1896), 280–282.

[15] A. Raczynski, *Les arts en Portugal* (Paris, 1846), p. 345, note.

[16] Vasconcellos, *Francisco de Hollanda* (Eitelbergers Quellenschriften, N.F., IX) (Vienna, 1899), cxlvi–cli.

[17] In *Giornale Arcadio*, CXIII, 357.

[18] G. Battelli, "Sansovino em Portugal," in *Ilustração Moderna*, IV (1929), 439.

[19] *Idem*, "Uma Lembrança de D. João II no Santuário de Sto. Antonio da Castanheiro," in *Ilustração Moderna*, v (1930), 221–222.

[20] *Idem*, "Sansovino em Portugal," in *Ilustração Moderna*, IV (1929), 437–440; "Sansovino, Terzi, e a Renascença Italiana em Portugal," in *Ilustração Moderna*, v (1930), 58–63.

[21] F. A. G. Teixeira, "Sansovino e Tomar," in *Ilustração Moderna*, IV (1929), 465–469; "A Ermida da Conceição em Tomar," in *Ilustração Moderna*, v (1930), 11–13.

[22] V. Correia, in *O Século*, Jan. 10, 1930.

[23] In *Ilustração Moderna*, v (1930), 341–345.

[24] Vasconcellos, "Sansovino," in *Ilustração Moderna*, v (1930), 119.

[25] Justi attributed this St. Jerome and two other painted terra-cotta works in the monastery of Belém to Sansovino. The others are a statue of the *Madonna* "of the type of Filippino Lippi," and a youthful *St. Leonard.* — C. Justi, "Die portugiesische Malerei des XVI Jahrhunderts," in *Preuss. Jahrb.*, 1888, p. 234.

[26] G. Bottari, *Raccolta di lettere sulla Pittura, Scultura, ed Architettura* (Rome, 1759), III, 333.

[27] F. Pérez Sedano, *Notas del archivio de la catedral de Toledo* (published by the Centro de Estudios Históricos, Madrid, 1914), p. 23. See also: C. R. Post, *A History of Spanish Painting* (Cambridge, Massachusetts, 1933), IV, 384.

[28] A. Haupt, *Geschichte der Renaissance in Spanien und Portugal* (Stuttgart, 1927), p. 26. O. Schubert, *Geschichte des Barock in Spanien* (Esslingen, 1908), p. 17.

CHAPTER III

[1] Giorgio Vasari, *Opere*, ed. Milanesi, VII (Florence, 1879), 153.

[2] One may doubt Vasari in this statement, since Soderini was not made Gonfaliere until the following year.

[3] Vasari, v, 350.

[4] C. von Fabriczy, document in *Preuss. Jahrb.*, 1906, pp. 86–88.

5 G. Milanesi, *Giornale Storico degli Archivi Toscani* (Florence, 1860), IV, 67 ff.

6 Archivio Gen. del Com. di Firenze: Rogiti di Giov. Franc. di Bernardo Bartoli dal M. S. Savino: Protocollo dal 1504 al 1513 @ 36.

7 Milanesi, *Giornale Storico degli Archivi Toscani*, IV, 66 ff.

8 Vasari, *Le Vite*, ed. C. Frey (Munich, 1911), p. 347.

9 *Idem, Opere*, VII, 488.

10 R. Borghini, *Il Riposo* (Reggio, 1926), bk. I, p. 135.

11 *Idem*, bk. IV, p. 59.

12 F. L. del Migliore, *Firenze, Città Nobilissima* (Florence, 1684), p. 91.

13 G. Richa, *Notizie istoriche delle chiese fiorentine*, V (Florence, 1757), xxii.

14 Follini, Rastrelli, *Firenze Antica e Moderna* (Florence, 1791), III, 30.

15 *Der Cicerone* (Basel, 1855), p. 640.

16 J. Burckhardt, *Der Cicerone*, ed. W. Bode, 5th edition (Paris, 1892), pt. II, p. 430.

17 H. Wölfflin, *The Art of the Italian Renaissance* (New York and London, 1913), p. 300.

18 Andrea Ferrucci had employed a similar disposition of Christ's hands in his relief of the Baptism which adorns the baptismal font of the cathedral of Pistoia. Date 1497–1499.

19 Cf. those two capitals in the sacristy vestibule of Sto. Spirito which differ from the rest, and the Doric portal in Monte San Savino.

20 G. Leoncini, *Illustrazione sulla cattedrale di Volterra* (Siena, 1869), p. 115.

21 G. Gaye, *Carteggio* (Florence, 1860), II, 62.

22 Santi Varno, *Di alcuni opere di Andrea Contucci da Monte San Savino scultore et architetto* (Genoa [Pagano], 1867).

23 Vasari, *Opere*, III, 466.

24 In *Preuss. Jahrb.*, 1909, p. 46.

CHAPTER IV

1 From:

E. Rodocanachi, *Le Pontificat de Jules II* (Histoire de Rome) (Paris, 1928).

Idem, Le Pontificat de Léon X (Histoire de Rome) (Paris, 1931).

J. Klaczko, *Jules II* (Paris, 1902).

E. Müntz, *Raphael* (London, 1882).

Idem, Histoire de l'Art pendant la Renaissance, II (Paris, 1891).

2 E. Mauceri, "Andrea Sansovino e i suoi scolari in Roma," in *L'Arte*, III (1900), 241.

3 This is demonstrated by Dr. Middeldorf: "Two Sansovino Drawings," in *Burlington Magazine*, 1934, pp. 107–115.

4 E. Bertaux, *Rome* (Paris, 1916), p. 7.

5 This possibility is suggested by C. R. Post, *A History of European and American Sculpture* (Cambridge, Massachusetts, 1921), I, 197.

6 The reclining figures below the relief panels on Ghiberti's later doors were constantly before the eyes of Florentine artists.

7 Cf. E. S. Prior and A. Gardner: *Medieval Figure Sculpture in England* (Cambridge, England, 1912), pp. 649–650; fig. 727. It is possible that Sansovino may have seen a tomb of the English type or even of English manufacture in Portugal. Portugal then, as now, was often closely leagued with England. Today Portugal contains many medieval alabaster altars that were made in England.

8 Notably the tomb of Martín Vázquez de Arce in the cathedral of Siguënza. A. Michel (editor), *Histoire de l'Arte*, vol. IV, pt. 2 (Paris, 1911), fig. 554.

[9] *The Renaissance in Italy*, v, "The Fine Arts," 155 ff.

[10] John Webster, *The Duchess of Malfi*, act IV, scene 2, lines 162–171.

[11] *Idem*, act III, scene 4, lines 1–2.

[12] B. Feliciangeli, "Documenti," in *Rassegna bibliografica dell'arte italiana*, 1915, pp. 115–117.

Julius II had announced his intention of erecting a tomb for Ascanio in a letter addressed to Gundisalvo Fernandi dated June 12, 1505. — Lib. brev. 22, @ 327[b], Secret Archives of the Vatican: L. Pastor, *History of the Popes* (New York, 1902), VI, 493 note.

[13] C. von Fabriczy, in *Preuss. Jahrb.*, 1906, pp. 101–102.

[14] Francesco Albertini, *Opusculum de mirabilibus novae et veteris urbis Romae* (Rome, 1510).

[15] Feliciangeli, "Salva condotti pontifici per Andrea Sansovino e Giuliano da S. Gallo," in *Rassegna bibliografica dell'arte italiana*, 1915, p. 117.

[16] Von Fabriczy, p. 98. Bode had recognized it as a work of Andrea Sansovino. See also: F. Schottmüller, *Die italienischen und spanischen Bildwerke der Renaissance und des Barocks* (Berlin, 1913), p. 161.

[17] Giorgio Vasari, *Opere*, ed. Milanesi, VII (Florence, 1879), 497.

[18] J. Burckhardt concurs in this opinion. Ref. *Der Cicerone* (Basel, 1855), p. 640.

[19] Müntz, *Raphael* (Paris, 1886), p. 297.

[20] Rodocanachi, *Le Pontificat de Jules II* (Histoire de Rome) (Paris, 1928), p. 89.

[21] Vasari, IV, 339.

[22] For a review of the *Coryciana* see the article by D. Gnoli in the *Rivista Italiana*, 1898.

[23] Burckhardt, *Der Cicerone*, ed. W. Bode, 5th edition (Paris, 1892), pt. II, p. 429. Müntz immediately refuted Bode's statement. See *Histoire de l'Art pendant la Renaissance*, p. 494.

CHAPTER V

[1] C. von Fabriczy, in *Preuss. Jahrb.*, 1906, pp. 88–89.

[2] Document III.

[3] The importance of this clause was pointed out by the writer of the recent anonymous article, "Andrea Sansovino a Loreto," in *Civiltà Cattolica*, 1931, p. 418.

[4] *Idem*, p. 419.

[5] Silvio Serragli, *La Santa Casa abbellita* (Macerata, 1634), p. 134.

[6] The above facts were drawn from the documents of the Santa Casa by the anonymous scholar writing in *Civ. Cat.*, 1931, p. 420.

[7] Document VI.

[8] F. dal Monte Casoni, *Il Santuario di Loreto e le sue difese militari* (Recanati, 1919), p. 153.

[9] "A. S. a L.," in *Civ. Cat.*, 1932, p. 19.

[10] Document VIII.

[11] Document IX.

[12] Document X.

[13] Document XI.

[14] Documents VI, VIII, IX, X, XI.

[15] *The Birth of Christ* is, it is needless to say, in reality an *Adoration of the Shepherds*.

[16] Document XVI.

[17] Document VIII.

[18] Document XII.

[19] *Idem.*

[20] Document XVI.

[21] Document X.

[22] Document XIII.

[23] Document XIV.

[24] "A. S. a L.," in *Civ. Cat.*, 1932, p. 229.

[25] Document XV.

[26] "A. S. a L.," in *Civ. Cat.*, 1932, p: 233.

[27] Document XVIII.

[28] "A. S. a L.," in *Civ. Cat.*, 1932, p. 233.

[29] C. Pini and G. Milanesi: *La Scrittura di artisti italiani* (Florence, 1869-1876), pl. III.

[30] "A. S. a L.," in *Civ. Cat.*, 1932, p. 235.

[31] Document XIX.

[32] Document VII.

[33] *Libro Mastro* "D" @ 85.

[34] Document XX.

[35] *Libro Mastro* "F" @ 31.

[36] Document VII. The account book contains entries for both 1517 and 1518.

[37] *Libri Mastri* "C" @ 80, "D" @ 68. Document XVII.

[38] "A. S. a L.," in *Civ. Cat.*, 1932, pp. 224-225.

[39] *Libro Mastro* "L" @ 70.

[40] *Libro Mastro* "K" @ 53, and @ 146. These documents are correctly summarized by G. Dossi, *Guida del viaggiatore alla città di Loreto* (Siena, 1895), pp. 131-132.

[41] *Idem*, pp. 132-133.

[42] *Idem*, p. 134.

[43] Gabinetto dei Disegni, Nos. 710, 710 esp., and 712 esp.

[44] Serragli, p. 132.

[45] Giorgio Vasari, *Opere*, ed. Milanesi, IV (Florence, 1879), 518-519.

[46] C. Frey and H. W. Frey, *Der literarische Nachlass Giorgio Vasaris* (Munich, 1930), II, 520.

[47] M. Reymond, *La Sculpture Florentine* (Florence, 1900), IV, 34.

[48] *Cod. Vat. Barb. Lat. 3 552*, cart. 34v. Quoted from E. Rodocanachi, *Le Pontificat de Léon X* (Histoire de Rome) (Paris, 1931), p. 159.

[49] "A. S. a L.," in *Civ. Cat.*, 1932, pp. 229-230.

[50] C. Frey, *Sammlung angewählter Briefe an Michelangelo Buonarroti* (Berlin, 1899), pp. 202-204.

[51] Vasari, IV, 521.

[52] *Idem*, p. 522.

[53] So, too, did von Fabriczy err (in *Preuss. Jahrb.*, 1906, pp. 94-95) when he maintained that the figure is carved of wood. Let him who doubts that it is terra-cotta try to lift it!

CHAPTER VI

[1] Giorgio Vasari, *Opere*, ed. Milanesi, IV (Florence, 1879), 511-512.

[2] Carlo Botto, "Edificazione della chiesa di Sto. Spirito in Firenze," in *Rivista d'Arte*, Oct. 1931, pp. 477-511; Jan. 1932, pp. 23-53.

[3] *Idem.*

[4] Document II.

[5] W. Stechow-Göttingen, "Zum plastischen Werk des Giuliano da San Gallo," in *Festschrift Schubrings* (Leipzig, 1929), pp. 138–143.

[6] U. Middeldorf, "Giuliano da San Gallo und Andrea Sansovino" in *Art Bulletin*, 1934, 107–115.

[7] Kupferstich Kabinett, No. 5624.

[8] Vasari, IV, 308.

[9] C. von Fabriczy, in *Preuss. Jahrb.*, 1906, p. 98. For plans and elevations of these two palaces see P. Letarouilly, *Les Édifices de Rome Moderne* (Liège, 1849), vol. II, pls. 153–156, 202–204.

[10] Vasari, VII, 497.

[11] Raffaele Erculei, "La Villa di Giulio III," in *Nuova Antologia*, 1890, pp. 83–106, esp. p. 88.

[12] Giacomo Balestra: *La Fontana Pubblica di Giulio III e il Palazzo di Pio IV sulla via Flaminia* (Rome, 1911). A more recent book with excellent illustrations and a good summary is *Il Palazzo di Pio IV sulla via Flaminia*, by Sante Bargellini and Ugo Jandolo (Milan and Rome, 1923).

[13] E. Müntz, *Histoire de l'Art pendant la Renaissance* (Paris, 1889–1895), II, 395.

[14] Document III.

[15] P. Gianuizzi, "La Chiesa di S. M. di Loreto," extracted from *La Rassegna Italiana* (Rome, 1884), p. 16.

[16] "A. S. a L.," in *Civiltà Cattolica*, 1931, p. 423.

[17] Vasari, IV, 522.

[18] "A. S. a L.," in *Civ. Cat.*, 1931, p. 425.

[19] Vasari, IV, 518.

[20] A. Gianandrea, *Il Palazzo del Commune di Jesi* (Jesi, 1887), p. 29.

[21] *Idem*, p. 30.

[22] Vasari, IV, 521.

[23] A. Gottschewski (editor), *Die Lebensbeschreibungen, etc. von G. Vasari* (Strassburg, 1904–1916), vol. VII, pt. I, pp. 90–122.

[24] Vasari, IV, 521.

[25] *Idem*.

[26] C. von Stegmann and H. von Geymüller, *Die Architectur der Renaissance in Toscana* (Munich, 1885–1908), IV, section B.

[27] *Idem*.

[28] U. Pasqui, *Nuova guida di Arezzo e de' suoi dintorni, compilata sui documenti* (Arezzo, 1882), p. 76.

[29] G. Mancini, *Guglielmo de Marcillat* (Florence, 1909), p. 43, n. 2.

[30] von Fabriczy, in *Preuss. Jahrb.*, 1906, pp. 91–92; Vasari, IV, 527.

CHAPTER VII

[1] See Bibliography.

[2] Uffizi, Gabinetto dei disegni, No. 14534.

[3] *Idem*, No. 14533.

[4] Giorgio Vasari, *Opere*, ed. Milanesi, IV (Florence, 1879), 523.

[5] "Two Sansovino Drawings," in *Burlington Magazine*, 1934, pp. 159–164.

[6] *Idem*.

[7] Cf. the buildings in certain reliefs by Ghirlandajo, notably the *Funeral of St. Francis* in Santa Trinita and *Joachim Driven from the Temple* in Santa Maria Novella.

[8] Jacopo Morelli, *Codici manoscritti della Libreria Naniana* (Venice, 1776), pp. 4, 5.

[9] Gabinetto dei disegni, Disegni architettonichi, Nos. 21, 2, 139, 141, 142.

APPENDIX I

[1] Giorgio Vasari, *Opere*, ed. Milanesi, IV (Florence, 1879), 510.

[2] *Idem.*

[3] *Idem.* The *Galba* has been restored to Vasari's house in recent years. See A. del Vita, in *Bolletino d'Arte*, 1919, pp. 30–32.

[4] This attribution was made by Dr. Ulrich Middeldorf, "Giuliano da Sangallo and Andrea Sansovino," in *Art Bulletin*, 1934, pp. 107–115.

[5] Document 1.

[6] U. Middeldorf, "Eine Zeichnung von Andrea Sansovino in München," in *Münch. Jahrb.*, N. F., x (1933), pp. 138–146.

[7] *Idem*, "Unknown Drawings of the Two Sansovinos," in the *Burlington Magazine*, 1932, pp. 236–245.

[8] Archivio Nazionale, Firenze, Convent 122, Cfr. No. 128 @ 199; also noted by von Fabriczy, in *Preuss. Jahrb.*, 1906, p. 96.

[9] Vasari, IV, 308.

[10] C. von Fabriczy, in *Preuss. Jahrb.*, 1906, p. 96, n. 1.

[11] Vasari, IV, 513.

[12] *Idem, Le Vite*, ed. C. Frey (Munich, 1911), I, 347.

[13] See above, Chapter II.

[14] Vasari, *Opere*, IV, 522. The head is in private possession in Montepulciano. I hope to get a photograph of it soon.

[15] *Idem*, p. 515, n. 1; G. Milanesi, *Giornale Storico degli Archivi Toscani*, IV (Florence, 1860), 66–67.

[16] Document published by G. Poggi, "Di un'opera di Andrea Sansovino del Palazzo della Signoria," in *Rivista d'Arte*, 1909, pp. 144–146.

[17] Documents: *Idem*; C. Frey, "Studien zu Michelagnolo Buonarroti und zur Kunst Seiner Zeit," in *Preuss. Jahrb.*, 1909, Beiheft, p. 126.

[18] G. Gaye, *Carteggio* (Florence, 1860), II, 62; Milanesi, *Sulla Storia dell'Arte Toscana* (Siena, 1873), pp. 250 ff.

[19] Vasari, *Opere*, VI, 625.

[20] In *Preuss. Jahrb.* 1906, p. 97. It is possible that Sansovino was appointed to the committee but did not serve on it.

[21] *Idem*, pp. 86–88.

[22] *Idem.*

[23] Milanesi, *Sulla Storia dell'Arte Toscana*, pp. 247–261; *Giornale Storico degli Archivi Toscani*, IV, 67.

[24] Archivio Notarile, Firenze, *Rogiti di Gio. Franco. di Bernardo Bartoli dal M. S. Savino*, Protocollo dal 1504 al 1513, @ 36.

[25] *Idem*, @ 45.

[26] B. Feliciangeli, "Documenti-Salvacondotti pontifici per Andrea Sansovino e Giuliano da S. Gallo," in *Rassegna bibliografica dell'arte italiana*, 1915, pp. 115–117.

[27] U. Mazzini, in *Giornale storico e letterario della Liguria*, 1904, p. 439; von Fabriczy, in *Preuss. Jahrb.*, 1906, pp. 101–102; F. Schottmüller, *Die italienischen und spanischen Bildwerke der Renaissance und des Barocks* (Berlin, 1913), p. 161.

[28] A. von Zahn, in *Archivio storico italiano*, VI, (1867), 180 (von Zahn read the date 1506); B. Feliciangeli, in *Rassegna bibliografica dell'arte italiana*, 1915, pp. 115–117; von Fabriczy, p. 102.

[29] G. Clausse, *Les San Gallo* (Paris, 1900), I, 236.

[30] von Fabriczy, in *Preuss. Jahrb.*, 1906, pp. 102–104.

[31] F. Albertini, *Opusculum de mirabilibus Novae et veteris Urbis Romae* (Rome, 1510).

[32] W. Bode, *Italienische Bildhauer der Renaissance* (Berlin, 1887), pp. 289 ff; von Fabriczy, in *Preuss. Jahrb.*, 1906, p. 98.

[33] Inscription:

> IESU DEO DEIQ. FILIO MATRI
> VIRGINI ANNAE AVIAE MATERNAE
> IO: CORICIUS EX GERMANIS
> LUCUMBURG. PROT. APOST. DDD.
> PERPETUO SACRIFICIO DOTEM
> VASA VESTES TRIBUIT MDXII

There are miniature bronze reproductions of this group in the Victoria and Albert Museum, London; in the collection of Lady Margaret Watney, England; and in the Palazzo Schifanoia, Ferrara.

[34] Vasari, *Opere*, IV, 527; von Fabriczy, in *Preuss. Jahrb.*, 1906, p. 89.

[35] Document III.

[36] "Andrea Sansovino a Loreto," in *Civiltà Cattolica*, 1931, p. 420.

[37] *Idem*, p. 419.

[38] Silvio Serragli, *La Santa Casa abbellita* (Macerata, 1634), p. 123.

[39] "A. S. a L.," in *Civ. Cat.*, 1931, p. 423, n. 1.

[40] *Idem*, p. 423.

[41] *Idem*, n. 2.

[42] Document IV.

[43] "A. S. a L." in *Civ. Cat.*, 1931, p. 421.

[44] *Idem*, p. 425.

[45] Vasari, *Opere*, VII, 188, 355.

[46] "A. S. a L.," in *Civ. Cat.*, 1931, p. 422.

[47] Archivio Notarile B 2364, Firenze, Rogiti di Brandino dal M. S. Savino, Protocollo dal 1515 al 1519 @ 19, @ 22.

[48] Vasari, *Opere*, IV, 527; von Fabriczy, in *Preuss. Jahrb.*, 1906, pp. 104-105.

[49] "A. S. a L.," in *Civ. Cat.*, 1932, p. 18.

[50] *Idem*, p. 424.

[51] *Idem*, p. 422.

[52] Document V.

[53] Document VI.

[54] "A. S. a L.," in *Civ. Cat.*, 1932, p. 16.

[55] C. von Stegmann and H. von Geymüller, *Die Architectur der Renaissance in Toscana* (Munich, 1885-1908), IV, section B.

[56] *Idem*; also Vasari, *Opere*, IV, 521 and VI, 300.

[57] "A. S. a L.," in *Civ. Cat.*, 1932, p. 18.

[58] Rogiti di Brandino, 1515-1519, @ 129, @ 146.

[59] Document VIII.

[60] A. Gianandrea, *Palazzo del Commune di Jesi* (Jesi, 1877), p. 29.

[61] "A. S. a L.," in *Civ. Cat.*, 1932, p. 19.

[62] Rogiti di Brandino, 1515-1519, @ 12, @ 14, @ 15, @ 30, @ 31.

[63] "A. S. a L.," in *Civ. Cat.*, 1932, p. 16.

[64] *Idem*, p. 19.

[65] Rogiti di Brandino, 1515-1519, @ 151, @ 156.

[66] Document IX.

[67] Document VIII.

[68] Document X.

[69] Document XII.

[70] Gianandrea, p. 29.

[71] "A. S. a L.," in *Civ. Cat.*, 1932, pp. 227–228.

[72] Document XII.

[73] Archivio Notarile B 2366, Firenze, Rogiti di Brandino dal M. S. Savino, Protocollo dal 1522 al 1525, @ 24, @ 25, @ 28, @ 31.

[74] Document XIII.

[75] Rogiti di Brandino, 1522–1525, @ 63, @ 69.

[76] Document XIV.

[77] Vasari, *Opere*, IV, 521.

[78] Rogiti di Brandino, 1522–1525, @ 73, @ 81, @ 118, @ 124, @ 125.

[79] Document XV.

[80] C. Pini and G. Milanesi, *La Scrittura di artisti italiani* (Florence, 1869–1876), vol. II; C. Frey, "Studien zu Michelagnolo," in *Preuss. Jahrb.*, 1896, pp. 99–101.

[81] Document XVI.

[82] Rogiti di Brandino, 1522–1525, @ 182, @ 191, @ 192, @ 196, @ 209.

[83] U. Pasqui: *Nuova guida di Arezzo e de' suoi dintorni, compilata sui documenti* (Arezzo, 1882), p. 76. But Girolamo Mancini (*Guglielmo de Marcillat* [Florence, 1909], p. 43, n. 2) maintained that these steps were designed by Guillaume de Marcillat. See also Vasari, *Opere*, IV, 522.

[84] "A. S. a L.," in *Civ. Cat.*, 1932, p. 234.

[85] *Idem.*

[86] *Idem*, n. 1.

[87] Rogiti di Brandino, 1522–1525, @ 83, @ 86, @ 89, @ 91, @ 96, @ 97, @ 99, @ 102.

[88] Document XVIII. Camillo is not on Milanesi's genealogical tree.

[89] *Idem.*

[90] "A. S. a L.," in *Civ. Cat.*, 1932, p. 235.

[91] Vasari, *Opere*, IV, 522.

[92] Rogiti di Brandino, 1522–1525, @ 186, @ 197.

[93] Von Fabriczy, in *Preuss. Jahrb.*, 1906, pp. 91–92; Vasari, *Opere*, IV, 527.

[94] Vasari, *Opere*, IV, 522.

[95] Von Fabriczy, in *Preuss. Jahrb.*, 1906, p. 100.

APPENDIX II

[1] The existence of this document was first noticed by Signor Carlo Botto in *Rivista d'Arte*, 1931, pp. 477–511; 1932, pp. 23–53. This is the first time it has been published.

[2] The dash represents illegible letters.

[3] Republished from C. von Fabriczy, "Simone del Pollaiuolo, Il Cronaca," in *Preuss. Jahrb.*, 1906, Beiheft, p. 52.

[4] Republished from "Andrea Sansovino a Loreto," in *Civiltà Cattolica*, 1931, pp. 427–428.

[5] From *idem*, p. 419.

[6] From *idem*, p. 429.

[7] From *idem*, p. 428.

[8] From *idem*, 1932, p. 224.

[9] The first five entries are from "A. S. a L.," in *Civ. Cat.*, 1932, p. 27. The last has never been fully published although the above article quotes a part of it (p. 19).

[10] From *idem*, pp. 20–21.

[11] From *idem*, p. 21.
[12] Previously unpublished.
[13] From *idem*, in *Civ. Cat.*, 1932, p. 28.
[14] From *idem*, p. 229.
[15] From *idem*, p. 230.
[16] From *idem*, pp. 231–232.
[17] From *idem*, p. 28.
[18] From *idem*, pp. 225–226.
[19] From *idem*, p. 29.
[20] Previously unpublished.
[21] Previously unpublished.

BIBLIOGRAPHY

BIBLIOGRAPHY

ABREU, M. "Sansovino," in *Ilustração Moderna*, 1930, p. 119.

ALBERTINI, F. *Memoriale di Molte Statue e Pitture della Città di Firenze*, Florence, 1510; reprinted, Florence, 1863, p. 16.
Opusculum de mirabilibus novae urbis Romae, Rome, 1510.

ALIZERI. *Notizie dei professori del disegno in Liguria*, vol. IV, pp. 271 ff.

"Andrea Sansovino a Loreto," in *Civiltà Cattolica*, December 5, 1931, pp. 415–429; January 2, 1932, pp. 15–29; February 6, 1932, pp. 223–236.

BATTELLI, G. In *Journal de Noticias*, December 28, 1929.
"A Capela dos Reis em S. Marcos," in *Ilustração Moderna*, 1930, pp. 8–10.
"A Chaminé de Sansovino no Paço Real de Sintra," in *Ilustração Moderna*, 1931, p. 254.
"Chaminés Italianas da Renascença," in *Ilustração Moderna*, 1931, pp. 291–293.
Il Sansovino in Portugallo, Coimbra, 1929.
"Sansovino em Portugal," in *Ilustração Moderna*, 1929, pp. 437–440.
"Sansovino, Terzi, e a Renascença Italiana em Portugal," in *Ilustração Moderna*, 1930, pp. 58–63.
"Uma Lembrança de D. João II no Santuário de Sto. Antonio da Castanheira," in *Ilustração Moderna*, 1930, pp. 221–222.

BELTRAMI, F. *Il Forestiere struito delle cose notabile della città di Ravenna*, Ravenna, 1791, p. 140.

BERTAUX, E. "La Renaissance en Espagne et en Portugal," in *Histoire de l'Art* (A. Michel, editor), vol. IV, part 2, Paris, 1911, pp. 817 ff.
Rome, Paris, 1916, p. 7.

BIEHL, W. "Ein unbekanntes Marmorbildwerk des Andrea Sansovino," in *Jahrbuch der Königlich Preuszischen Kunstsammlungen*, 1915, pp. 129 ff.

BOCCHI-CINELLI. *Le bellezze di Firenze*, Pistoìa, 1678.

BODE, W. Review of Schönfeld's *Andrea Sansovino und seine Schule* in *Repertorium für Kunstwissenschaft*, 1881, p. 311.
"Die Italienischen Skulpturen der Renaissance in den königlichen Museen zu Berlin," in *Jahrbuch der Königlich Preuszischen Kunstsammlungen*, 1886, p. 34.
Italienische Bildhauer der Renaissance, Berlin, 1887, pp. 289 ff.
(editor) *Le Cicerone*, by J. Burckhardt, fifth edition, translated by A. Gerard, Paris, 1892, part II, pp. 428–430.

BORGHINI. *Il Riposo*, reprinted, Reggio, 1826.

BOTTARI. *Raccolta di lettere sulla Pittura, Scultura, ed Architettura*, Rome, 1759, vol. III, p. 333.

BOTTO, CARLO. "L'edificazione della chiesa di Santo Spirito, in Firenze," in *Rivista d'Arte*, 1931, pp. 477–511; 1932, pp. 23–53.

BROGI, F. *Inventario generale degli oggetti d'arte della provincia di Siena*, Siena, 1897, p. 250.

BURCKHARDT, J. *Der Cicerone*, Basel, 1855, pp. 639–641.

BURGER, F. *Geschichte des Florentinischen Grabmals*, Strassburg, 1904.

CAROCCI, G.   "Di alcune opere di Andrea Sansovino," in *Arte e Storia*, 1912, pp. 249–252.
  Schedario Carocci, Com. 11, edif. 4, schede 3, Mss. in S. Marco, Florence.

CARUSO, G.   "Andrea Contucci detto il Sansovino nelle sue opere in Rome," in *Capitolum*, 1929, pp. 149–152.

CLAUSSE, G.   *Les San Gallo*, Paris, 1900.

CORREIA, V.   In *O Século*, January 10, 1930.
  A Escultura em Portugal, no primeiro terço do século XVI, Coimbra, 1929 (extracted from *Arte e Arqueologia*, vol. I, No. 1)

Coryciana, by friends of Johann Goritz, Rome, 1524.

CRUICKSHANK, J. W. and A. M.   *The Smaller Tuscan Towns*, London, 1912.

CRUTTWELL, M.   *Antonio Pollajuolo*, London and New York, 1907.

DAVIES, G. S.   *Renaissance Tombs of Rome*, London, 1910, pp. 171–176, 303–305.

DOSSI, G. P.   *Guida del viaggiatore alla città di Loreto*, Siena, 1895.

ERCULEI, R.   "La Villa di Giulio III," in *Nuova Antologia*, 1890, pp. 83–106.

FABIANI, F.   *Andrea Sansovino*, Rome, 1864.

VON FABRICZY, C. (editor).   *Der Cicerone*, by J. Burckhardt, Leipzig.
  "Ein unbekanntes Jugendwerk Andrea Sansovinos," in *Jahrbuch der Königlich Preuszischen Kunstsammlungen*, 1906, pp. 79–105.
  "Kritisches Verzeichnis Toskanischer Holz– und Tonstatuen," in *Jahrbuch der Königlich Preuszischen Kunstsammlungen*, 1909, Beiheft, pp. 16, 24, 28, 39, 46, 47, 52, 53, 126.
  "Simone del Pollaiuolo, il Cronaca," in *Jahrbuch der Königlich Preuszischen Kunstsammlungen*, 1906, Beiheft, pp. 45–69.

FELICIANGELI, B.   "Salvacondotti pontificii per Andrea Sansovino e Giuliano da S. Gallo," in *Rassegna Bibliografica dell'arte italiana*, 1915, pp. 115–117.

FERRI, N.   *Catalogo riassuntivo della Raccolta di Disegni degli Uffizi di Firenze*, Florence, 1897.

FISCHER, A.   In *Zeitschrift für bildende Kunst*, 1879, pp. 149–152.

FOLLINI, RASTRELLI.   *Firenze Antica e Moderna*, Florence, 1791, vol. III, p. 30.

FORATTI, A.   "Un arco Sansovinesco a Montagrana," in *Arte e Storia*, 1911, pp. 139–141.

FRASCHETTI, S.   "Le rappresentazioni allegoriche nei monumenti romani della rinascenza," in *Emporium*, 1902, p. 109.

FREEMAN, L. J.   *Italian Sculpture of the Renaissance*, New York, 1901.

FREY, C.   *Briefe an Michelangelo*, Berlin, 1899.
  Der literarische Nachlass Giorgio Vasaris, Munich, 1923, vol I.
  (editor) *Le Vite, scritte da M. Giorgio Vasari*, Munich, vol. I, 1911, p. 347.
  Sammlung ausgewählter Briefe an Michelangelo, Berlin, 1899, p. 203.
  "Studien zu Michelagnolo," in *Jahrbuch der Königlich Preuszischen Kunstsammlungen*, 1896, pp. 99–101.
  "Studien zu Michelagnolo Buonarroti und zur Kunst seiner Zeit," in *Jahrbuch der Königlich Preuszischen Kunstsammlungen*, 1909, Beiheft, p. 126.

FREY, C. and HERMAN-WALTHER.   *Der Literarische Nachlass Giorgio Vasaris*, Munich, vol. II, 1930, pp. 520–521.

GAYE, GIOVANNI.   *Carteggio*, Florence, 1860, vol. II, p. 62; vol. III, p. 119.

GIANANDREA, A.   *Il Palazzo del Comune di Jesi*, Jesi, 1887, pp. 29–30.

GIANUIZZI, P. "Documenti inedite sulla Basilica Loretana," in *Archivio Storico dell-'Arte*, 1888, pp. 273–276, 321–327, 364–369, 415–424, 451–453.
"La chiesa di S. Maria di Loreto," in *La Rassegna Italiana*, 1884; also extracted and printed separately, Rome, 1884, p. 16.

GIOVANNONI, G. "Un' opera sconosciuta di Jacopo Sansovino in Roma," in *Bolletino d'Arte*, 1917, pp. 64–81.

GNOLI, D. *Have Roma*, Rome, 1909, p. 169.

GOTTI, A. *Storia del Palazzo Vecchio*, Florence, 1889, p. 114.

GOTTSCHEWSKI, A. (editor). *Die Lebensbeschreibungen, etc., von G. Vasari*, translated by Gottschewski, Gronau, and Jasche, Strassburg, 1904–1916.

GRUYER, G. *L'Art Ferrarais*, Paris, 1897, pp. 530–531.

HAUPT, A. *Die Baukunst der Renaissance in Portugal*, Frankfurt a. M., 1890.
Geschichte der Renaissance in Spanien und Portugal (in the series of "Neueren Baukunst,") Stuttgart, 1927, pp. 26, 154.

JUSTI, C. "Die Portugiesche Malerei des XVI Jahrhunderts," in *Jahrbuch der Königlich Preuszischen Kunstsammlungen*, 1888, p. 234.
Michelangelo, Berlin, 1908, p. 133.
Miscellaneen aus Dreihunderten Jahren Spanischen Kunstlebens, Berlin, 1908.

KALLAB, W. *Vasaristudien*, Vienna and Leipzig, 1908.

KLACZKO, J. *Jules II*, Paris, 1902.

LAMPORI. *Cataloghi ed Inventari inediti*, Modena, 1870, p. 192.

LEONCINI, G. *Illustrazione sulla cattedrale di Volterra*, Siena, 1869, p. 115.

LETAROUILLY, P. *Les édifices de Rome moderne*, Liège, 1849.

LUMACHI, A. *Memoirie storiche di Giovanni Battista di Firenze*, Florence, 1782, p. 112.

MANCINI, G. *Cortona, Montecchio, Vesponi e Castiglione Fiorentino* (Italia Artistica, No. 46), Bergamo, 1909, pp. 156–157, 166.
Guglielmo de Marcillat, Florence, 1909, p. 33, note 1; p. 43, note 2.
La Vita di Luca Signorelli, Florence, 1903, p. 63, note 3.

MARCHIO. *Il forrestiere informato delle cose di Lucca*, Lucca, 1721, p. 282.

MARQUAND, A. *Andrea della Robbia*, vol. II, Princeton, 1922.
Giovanni della Robbia, Princeton, London, Oxford, 1920.

MAUCERI, E. "Andrea Sansovino e i suoi scolari in Roma," in *L'Arte*, 1900, pp. 241–258.

MAURO, L. *Le antichità della città di Roma* (contains: U. Aldroandi, *Tutte le Statue antiche che in Roma in diversi luoghi e case particulari si veggono raccolte e descritte*), Venice, 1556.

MAZZINI. In *Giornale storico e letterario della Liguria*, 1904, pp. 438–440.

MELCHIORRI. *Guida di Roma*, p. 584.

MIDDELDORF, U. "Eine Zeichnung von Andrea Sansovino in München," in *Münchner Jahrbuch der Bildenden Kunst*, N.F. X, 1933, pp. 138–146.
"Giuliano da Sangallo and Andrea Sansovino," in *Art Bulletin*, 1934, pp. 107–115.
"Unknown Drawings of the Two Sansovinos," in *Burlington Magazine*, 1932, pp. 236–245.
"Two Sansovino Drawings," in *Burlington Magazine*, 1934, pp. 159–164.

MIGLIORE, F. L. DA. *Florence, Città Nobilissima*, Florence, 1684, p. 91.

MILANESI, G. *Giornale Storico degli Archivi Toscani*, vol. IV, Florence, 1860, pp. 66–67.
  Le Lettere di Michelangelo Buonarroti, Florence, 1875, p. 620.
  (editor) *Le opere di Giorgio Vasari*, Florence, 1878–1885, nine volumes.
  Miscellanee, Mss. in the Library, Siena.
  Sulla storia dell' Arte toscana scritti vari, Siena, 1873, pp. 250 ff.

MONTE CASONI, F. DAL. *Il Santuario di Loreto e le sue difesi militari*, Recanati, 1919, p. 153.

MORELLI, J. *Codici manoscritti della Libreria Naniana*, Venice, 1776, pp. 14–15.

MÜNTZ, E. *Histoire de l'Art pendant la Renaissance*, Paris, 1889–1895.
  Raphael, London, 1882.

NIBBY, ANTONIO. In *Giornale Arcadio di Roma*, vol. CXVIII, p. 357.

PASQUI, U. *Nuova guida di Arezzo e de' suoi dintorni, compilata sui documenti*, Arezzo, 1882, p. 76.

PERKINS, C. C. *Historical Handbook of Italian Sculpture*, New York, 1883.
  Tuscan Sculptors, London, 1864.

PINI, C. and MILANESI, G. *La Scrittura di artisti italiani*, Florence, 1869–1876, plate III.

PITTONI, L. "Di alcune opere Sansovinesche," in *Rassegna d'Arte*, 1909, pp. 187–189.
  Jacopo Sansovino scultore, Venice, 1909.

PLANISCIG, L. *Venezianische Bildhauer der Renaissance*, Vienna, 1921.

POGGI, GIOVANNI. "Di un 'opera di Andrea Sansovino del Palazzo della Signoria," in *Rivista d'Arte*, 1909, pp. 144–146.

POST, C. R. *A History of European and American Sculpture*, Cambridge, 1921.

RACZYNSKI, A. *Les arts en Portugal*, Paris, 1846.

RASTEIRO, J. *Quinta e Palacio de Bacalhoa em Azeitão*, Lisbon, 1895 and 1898.

REYMOND, M. *La sculpture florentine*, Florence, 1897–1900.

RICCI, C. *Mostra Sanese*, Bergamo, 1904, ill. 126.

RICHA, G. *Notizie istoriche delle chiese fiorentine*, Florence, vol. V, 1757, p. xxii; vol. IX, 1761, pp. 26, 32.

RIDOLFI, E. *Guida di Lucca*, Lucca, 1899, p. 155.

RODOCANACHI, E. *Le Pontificat de Jules II* (Histoire de Rome), Paris, 1928.
  Le Pontificat de Léon X (Histoire de Rome), Paris, 1931.

ROGGE, T. "Ein Palast Andrea Sansovino's in Portugal," in *Zeitschrift für bildende Kunst*, 1896, pp. 280–282.

ROSENBERG, A. "Andrea Sansovino," in *Kunst und Kunstler*, Leipzig, 1879, pp. 3–14.

DEL ROSSO. *Ricerchi storichi attorno del Battistero*, Florence, 1820, p. 73.

SCHMARSOW, A. "Ein Entwurf Michelangelo's zum Grabmal Julius' II," in *Jahrbuch der Königlich Preuszischen Kunstsammlungen*, 1884, p. 69.

SCHÖNFELD, P. *Andrea Sansovino und seine Schule*, Stuttgart, 1881.

SCHOTTMÜLLER, F. *Die italienischen und spanischen Bildwerke der Renaissance und des Barocks* (Königliche Museen zu Berlin), Berlin, 1913.

SCHUBERT, O. *Geschichte des Barock in Spanien*, Esslingen, 1908.

SEMPER, H. and BARTH W. *Bildhauer-Architekten der Renaissance*, Dresden, 1880, pp. 9–16.

SERRAGLI, SILVIO. *La S. Casa abbellita*, Macerata, 1634.

STECHOW–GÖTTINGEN, W. "Zum Plastischen Werk des Giuliano da San Gallo," in *Festschrift Schubring*, Leipzig, 1929, pp. 138–143.

VON STEGMANN, C. and VON GEYMÜLLER, H. *Die Architektur der Renaissance in Toscana*, Munich, 1885–1908, vol. IV, section B.

SYMONDS, J. A. *The Renaissance in Italy*, vol. V, "The Fine Arts," New York, 1888.

VON TSCHUDI, H. "Giovanni Dalmata," in *Jahrbuch der Königlich Preuszischen Kunstsammlungen*, 1883, pp. 180, 187.

TEIXEIRA, F. A. G. "A Ermida da Conceçião em Tomar," in *Ilustração Moderna*, 1930, pp. 11–13.
"Sansovino e Tomar," in *Ilustração Moderna*, 1929, pp. 465–469.

TRENTA, T. *Guida pel forestiere per la città e il contado di Lucca*, Lucca, 1820, p. 105.

VARNI, S. *Di alcune opere di Andrea Contucci da monte San Savino scultore ed architetto*, Genoa, 1867.

VASARI, G. *Le Opere* (edition G. Milanesi), Florence, 1878–1885, nine volumes.
Le Vite (first edition), Florence, 1550; republished by C. Ricci, Milan and Rome (no date).
Le Vite (second edition), Florence, 1568; republished by Bottari, Rome, 1759.

VASCONCELLOS, J. de *Francisco de Hollanda* (Eitelbergers Quellenschriften, N.F., vol. IX), Vienna, 1899, pp. cxlvi–cli.

VENTURI, A. In *Archivio Storico dell'Arte*, 1888, p. 107.
La Madonna, Milan, 1900, p. 53.

DELLA VITA, A. "Di una Ceramica di Andrea Sansovino," in *Bolletino d'Arte*, 1919, pp. 30–32.

VOGEL. *De Ecclesia Recanatensi et Lauretana Commentarius historicus*, Recanati, 1859, vol. I, p. 313.

DE VORAGINE, JACOBUS. *La Légende Dorée* (edition J.-B. M. Roze), Paris, 1902.

WATSON, W. C. *Portuguese Architecture*, London, 1908.

WÖLFFLIN, H. *The Art of the Italian Renaissance*, New York and London, 1913.

VON ZAHN A. (editor). *Der Cicerone*, by J. Burckhardt, Leipzig, 1874, vol. II, pp. 692–695.
"Notizie artistiche tratte dall'archivio segreto vaticano," in *Archivio storico italiano*, Series III, vol. VI, Florence, 1867, p. 180.

INDEX

INDEX

(The most important citations of the works of Sansovino are given in
italicized numerals.)

FIG. 1. ANDREA SANSOVINO: HEAD OF GALBA
HOUSE OF GIORGIO VASARI, AREZZO. (*Glazed terra-cotta*)

Fototeca Italiana

Fig. 2. ANDREA SANSOVINO: ALTAR OF THE MADONNA AND SAINTS

S. Chiara, Monte San Savino. (*Glazed terra-cotta*)

Photograph: Alinari

Fig. 3. ANDREA SANSOVINO: TABERNACLE OF THE OIL

S. Margherita in Montici, near Florence. (*Marble*)

Fig. 4. ANDREA SANSOVINO: CHERUBIN

TABERNACLE OF THE OIL, S. MARGHERITA IN MONTICI, NEAR FLORENCE

FIG. 5. ANDREA SANSOVINO: LEFT ANGEL

TABERNACLE OF THE OIL, S. MARGHERITA IN MONTICI, NEAR FLORENCE

Fig. 6. ANDREA SANSOVINO: RIGHT ANGEL

Tabernacle of the Oil, S. Margherita in Montici, near Florence

Fig. 7. ANDREA SANSOVINO: ALTAR OF THE SACRAMENT

Corbinelli Chapel, S. Spirito, Florence. (*Marble*)

Photograph: Alinari

Fɪɢ. 8. ANDREA SANSOVINO: ALTAR OF THE SACRAMENT (*Reconstructed*)

S. Spirito, Florence

Photograph: Brogi

FIG. 9.   ANDREA SANSOVINO: THE CHRIST CHILD AND THE CORONATION OF THE VIRGIN

ALTAR OF THE SACRAMENT, S. SPIRITO, FLORENCE

Photograph: Alinari

Fig. 10. ANDREA FERRUCCI: ALTAR–PIECE FROM S. GIROLAMO, FIESOLE

Victoria and Albert Museum, London. (*Marble*)

Photograph: Victoria and Albert Museum

FIG. 11.   ANDREA SANSOVINO: GABRIEL, ST. MATTHEW, AND THE
DECOLLATION OF ST. MATTHEW

ALTAR OF THE SACRAMENT, S. SPIRITO, FLORENCE

Photograph: Alinari

FIG. 12. ANDREA SANSOVINO: VIRGIN ANNUNCIATE, ST. JAMES,
AND A MIRACLE OF ST. JAMES

ALTAR OF THE SACRAMENT, S. SPIRITO, FLORENCE

Photograph: Alinari

FIG. 13. ANDREA SANSOVINO: THE DECOLLATION OF ST. MATTHEW. (*Detail*)

ALTAR OF THE SACRAMENT, S. SPIRITO, FLORENCE

FIG. 14. ANDREA SANSOVINO: THE DECOLLATION OF ST. MATTHEW. (*Detail*)
ALTAR OF THE SACRAMENT, S. SPIRITO, FLORENCE

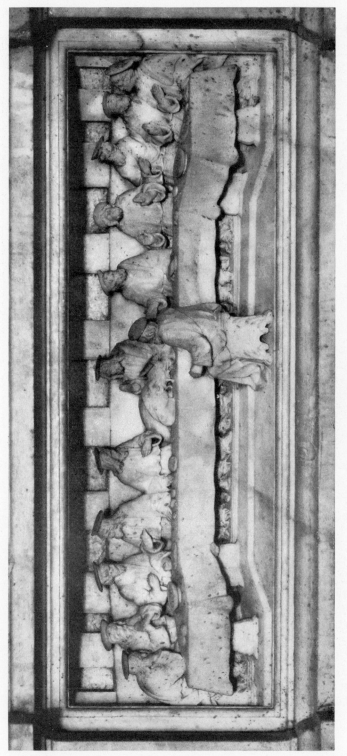

Fig. 15. ANDREA SANSOVINO: THE LAST SUPPER

Altar of the Sacrament, S. Spirito, Florence

Courtesy of Dr. Middledorf

FIG. 16. ANDREA SANSOVINO: THE PIETÀ
ALTAR OF THE SACRAMENT, S. SPIRITO, FLORENCE

Photograph: Brogi

FIG. 17. ANDREA SANSOVINO: HEAD OF ST. JOHN THE EVANGELIST. (*Detail of the Pietà*)
ALTAR OF THE SACRAMENT, S. SPIRITO, FLORENCE

Fig. 18. ANDREA SANSOVINO: ALTAR OF ST. LAWRENCE

S. Chiara, Monte San Savino. (*Painted terra-cotta*)

Photograph: Alinari

FIG. 19. ANDREA SANSOVINO: SAINT

ALTAR OF ST. LAWRENCE, S. CHIARA, MONTE SAN SAVINO

Fig. 20.   ANDREA SANSOVINO: ST. ROCH VISITS THE PLAGUE-STRICKEN

Altar of St. Lawrence, S. Chiara, Monte San Savino

Fig. 21. ANDREA SANSOVINO: ALTAR OF ST. LAWRENCE. (*Oblique view*)

S. Chiara, Monte San Savino

FIG. 22. VILLA OF BACALHOA EM AZEITÃO

RIBATEJO, PORTUGAL

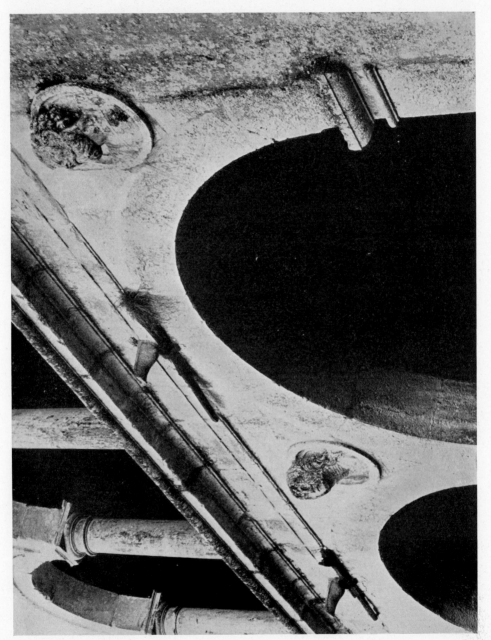

Fig. 23. NORTH LOGGIA. (*Detail*)

Villa of Bacalhoa

Fig. 24. CEILING OF ROOM ON GROUND FLOOR. (*Detail*)

VILLA OF BACALHOA

Fig. 25. TANK AND GARDEN LOGGIA

Villa of Bacalhoa

FIG. 26. ST. JEROME

MONASTIC CHURCH OF BELEM, NEAR LISBON. (*Painted terra-cotta*)

Courtesy: Marques Abreu

FIG. 27. ANDREA SANSOVINO: MADONNA AND CHILD

BARGELLO, FLORENCE. (*Terra-cotta*)

Photograph: Brogi

Fig. 28. ANDREA SANSOVINO: ST. JOHN BAPTIZING CHRIST

S. Giovanni, Florence. (*Marble*)

Photograph: Alinari

FIG. 29. ANDREA SANSOVINO AND INNOCENZO SPINAZZI: ST. JOHN BAPTIZING CHRIST, AND ATTENDANT ANGEL.
BAPTISTRY, FLORENCE. (*Marble*)

Photograph: Alinari

Fig. 30. ANDREA SANSOVINO: BAPTISMAL FONT

Baptistry, Volterra. (*Marble*)

Photograph: Brogi

Fig. 31. ANDREA SANSOVINO: JUSTICE
Baptismal Font, Baptistry, Volterra

FIG. 32. ANDREA SANSOVINO: ST. JOHN THE BAPTIST
CHAPEL OF ST. JOHN THE BAPTIST, CATHEDRAL, GENOA. (*Marble*)

Photograph: Alinari

FIG. 33. ANDREA SANSOVINO: MADONNA AND CHILD

CHAPEL OF ST. JOHN THE BAPTIST, CATHEDRAL, GENOA. (*Marble*)

Photograph: Alinari

Fig. 34. ANDREA SANSOVINO: ST. ANTHONY ABBOT

S. Andrea, Lucca. (*Painted wood*)

Fig. 35. ANDREA SANSOVINO: ST. ANTHONY ABBOT. (*Detail*)

S. Andrea, Lucca

Fig. 36. ANDREA SANSOVINO: ST. MATTHEW. (*Detail*)
Altar of the Sacrament, S. Spirito, Florence. (*Marble*)

FIG. 37. ANDREA SANSOVINO: TOMB OF CARDINAL SFORZA

S. MARIA DEL POPOLO, ROME. (*Marble*)

Photograph: Anderson

Fig. 38. ANDREA SANSOVINO: TOMB OF CARDINAL BASSO

S. Maria del Popolo, Rome. (*Marble*)

FIG. 39.   ANDREA SANSOVINO: JUSTICE

TOMB OF CARDINAL SFORZA, S. MARIA DEL POPOLO, ROME

Photograph: Anderson

Fig. 40. ANDREA SANSOVINO: HOPE

Tomb of Cardinal Sforza, S. Maria del Popolo, Rome

Photograph: Anderson

FIG. 41. ANDREA SANSOVINO: ARABESQUE

TOMB OF CARDINAL BASSO, S. MARIA DEL POPOLO, ROME

FIG. 42. ANDREA SANSOVINO: TOMB OF CARDINAL BASSO

S. Maria del Popolo, Rome. (*Marble*)

Photograph: Alinari

Fig. 43. ANDREA SANSOVINO: FORTITUDE

Tomb of Cardinal Basso, S. Maria del Popolo, Rome

FIG. 44. ANDREA SANSOVINO: TEMPERANCE
TOMB OF CARDINAL BASSO, S. MARIA DEL POPOLO, ROME

FIG. 45. TOMB OF CARDINAL DE' VINCENTI

S. MARIA IN ARACOELI, ROME. (*Marble*)

Photograph: Anderson

Fig. 46. ANDREA SANSOVINO: MADONNA AND CHILD AND TWO SOULS
S. Maria dell'Anima, Rome. (*Marble*)

Inscription on statue base:

IESV·DEO·DEIQ·FILIO·MATRI
VIRGINI·ANNÆ·AVIÆ·MATERNÆ·
IO·CORICIVS·EX·GERMANIS
LVCVMBVRG·PROT·APOST·DDD·
PERPETVO·SACRIFICIO·DOTEM
VASA·VESTES·TRIBVIT·MDXII

Fɪɢ. 47. ANDREA SANSOVINO: ST. ANNE, THE VIRGIN, AND CHILD
S. Aɢᴏsᴛɪɴᴏ, Rᴏᴍᴇ. (*Marble*)

Photograph: Luce

FIG. 48. ANDREA SANSOVINO: HEAD OF THE VIRGIN

St. Anne, the Virgin, and Child. S. Agostino, Rome

Photograph: Sansaini

Fig. 49. DONATO BRAMANTE, ANDREA SANSOVINO, AND OTHERS: THE SANTA CASA

Loreto. (*Marble*)

Photograph: Alinari

FIG. 50. ANDREA SANSOVINO: THE ANNUNCIATION

THE SANTA CASA, LORETO

Photograph: Alinari

Fig. 51. ANDREA SANSOVINO: THE ADORATION OF THE SHEPHERDS

The Santa Casa, Loreto

Photograph: Alinari

FIG. 52. ANDREA SANSOVINO AND IL TRIBOLO: THE MARRIAGE OF THE VIRGIN

THE SANTA CASA, LORETO

Photograph: Alinari

Fig. 53. ANDREA SANSOVINO: MADONNA AND CHILD
S. Maria in Porta Paradisi, Rome. (*Marble*)

FIG. 54. ANDREA SANSOVINO: ST. ROCH

S. QUIRICO, BATTIFOLLE, NEAR AREZZO. (*Painted terra-cotta*)

Fototeca Italiana

Fig. 55. ANDREA SANSOVINO: ST. ROCH. (*Detail*)

S. Quirico, Battifolle, near Arezzo

FIG. 56. ANDREA SANSOVINO: CAPITAL

SACRISTY, S. SPIRITO, FLORENCE. (*Pietra serena*)

Photograph: Alinari

FIG. 57. ANDREA SANSOVINO AND GIULIANO DA SAN GALLO: ANTESACRISTY

S. SPIRITO, FLORENCE

Photograph: Brogi

FIG. 58. ANDREA SANSOVINO: COURTYARD OF THE PALAZZO DEL COMUNE
JESI

FIG. 59. ANDREA SANSOVINO: LOWER PIERS

COURTYARD OF THE PALAZZO DEL COMUNE, JESI

Fig. 60. ANDREA SANSOVINO: ARCHES OF PRINCIPAL FLOOR
Courtyard of the Palazzo del Comune, Jesi

Fig. 61. ANDREA SANSOVINO: SANSOVINO'S HOUSE

Monte San Savino

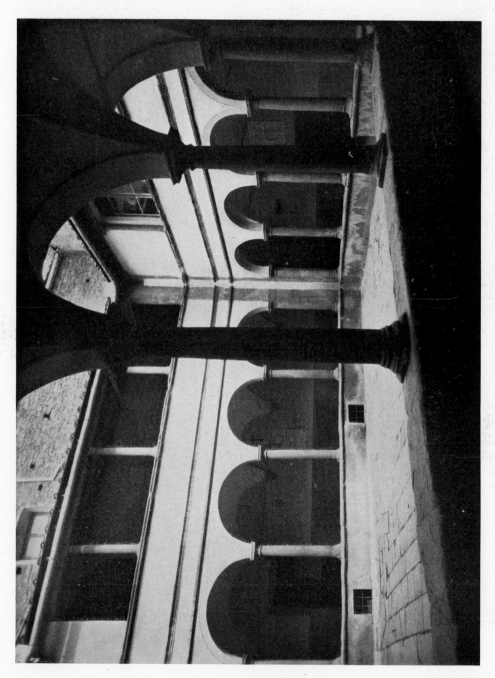

Fig. 62. ANDREA SANSOVINO: CLOISTER OF S. AGOSTINO

Monte San Savino

Fig. 67. ANDREA SANSOVINO: ST. JOSEPH RESTING

Uffizi, Florence. (*Pencil drawing*)

Fototeca Italiana

FIG. 68. ANDREA SANSOVINO: ASTRONOMY

UFFIZI, FLORENCE. (*Pencil drawing*)

Fototeca Italiana

FIG. 69. ANDREA SANSOVINO: DESIGN FOR AN ALTAR

MUNICH. (*Pen drawing*)

Photograph: Munich Museum

Fig. 70. ANDREA SANSOVINO: DESIGN FOR A TOMB

Victoria and Albert Museum, London. (*Pen drawing*)

Photograph: Victoria and Albert Museum

FIG. 71. ANDREA SANSOVINO: DESIGN FOR A TOMB

WEIMAR (*Pen drawing*)

Photograph: Braun

FIG. 72. ANDREA SANSOVINO: DESIGN FOR THE TOMB OF LEO X

VICTORIA AND ALBERT MUSEUM, LONDON. (*Pen drawing*)

Photograph: Victoria and Albert Museum

FIG. 73. ANDREA SANSOVINO: ARCHITECTURAL STUDY

UFFIZI, FLORENCE. (*Pen drawing*)

Photograph: Alinari